A Practical Legal Guide for Tourists and Business Travelers

Dominican Republic

By Michael L. Moore Esq.

DEDICATION

This book is dedicated to the memory of my late older brother, Kenneth Lee Moore, whose tragic murder at 15 years of age inspired me to write this series of books.

This book is also dedicated to my parents, John Henry Moore, and Edna Mae Moore, whose tremendous parenting skills kept me focused on the important things in life: being reverent, getting educated, and prioritizing family.

Finally, this book is dedicated to my beautiful family, my wife Royellen, my son AJ, and my daughter Karla. They inspire me every single day to be kind, patient, and compassionate.

IN LOVING MEMORY OF:

Belinda Joyce Moore Moss—my beautiful and wonderful sister, who supported me in every positive thing that I ever attempted to do.

Michael Eugene Baker—my dedicated and loyal friend and brother, who always wanted the very best for me.

Sylvia Joyce Hill—my eldest sister, who had a beautiful spirit and was like a second mother to me.

LAW OF THE LAND ®
PUBLISHING for Tourists & Business Travelers

Travel smart. Stay legal. Stay safe.®

From local laws to medical guides we've got you covered world wide
in one digital platform.

Travel Safe Anywhere
3 MONTHS FREE TRIAL

SCAN QR code
for more info

PREFACE

My introduction to the justice system came when I was only 10 years old. My 15-year-old brother was murdered with a butcher knife by a 19-year-old in a simple argument over a torn shirt. I was devastated by his death and sought retribution for his fate that never came. The woman was initially charged with second degree murder, but after plea negotiations, she was convicted of manslaughter and sentenced to only five years in a youthful offender school and ordered to undergo psychiatric care. That was it. Nothing more. The judicial system had run its course.

My family knew nothing about the justice system, and we did not have the tools to advocate for ourselves. No one provided us with a written source to reference for guidance through this process. There was no easily accessible, easy to understand, definitive source to educate ourselves about the legal system that we suddenly and unexpectedly found ourselves immersed in after being victimized by such a violent criminal act.

As I got older, finished college, law school, and ultimately started practicing law, it became clear to me that most people are not knowledgeable about the law or how the judicial process works. If most people are uninformed here in the United States regarding the law and the legal process, how would they fare when in other countries? I realized that tourists and businesspeople who travel internationally needed access to information on how to navigate the legal system in other countries!

For many years, there has been considerable media attention focused on international travelers experiencing legal difficulties while traveling abroad. Most of these news stories gained attention in the United States and abroad because they involved American citizens facing punishment that was considered "unconventional" and "harsh" by United States' legal standards. I recall a news story in 1994 regarding Michael Fay, a young American male, who had broken the law in Singapore. He was convicted and sentenced to be caned and or whipped publicly. While the United States Government weighed in on the inappropriate and cruel nature of the punishment, the young American was beaten because he had been convicted under Singapore law.

Similarly, in recent years, international news stories have garnered headlines regarding foreign travelers and their issues with the laws of countries that were not their own. Amanda Knox, an American woman, was accused of murdering her roommate in Italy in 2007 and spent almost four years in an Italian prison before being definitively acquitted by the Supreme Court of Cassatio. Kenneth Bae, an American citizen, was arrested in North Korea in 2012 and was convicted for hostile acts against the communist country. He was sentenced to 15 years hard labor but was released in 2014 after efforts by the U.S. State Department. More recently, United States Basketball Star, Brittany Griner was arrested in February 2022 at a Moscow airport on drug-related charges and detained for nearly 10 months, spending much of that time in prison. Her plight unfolded at the same time Russia invaded Ukraine and further heightened tensions between Russia and the United States, ending only after she was freed in exchange for a notorious Russian arms dealer.

It was in 1994 that another personal tragic event occurred that finally inspired me to write these series of books. A dear friend and also client of mine was brutally murdered while on his second honeymoon in Jamaica. News of his murder shocked me and our local community. The legal hurdles his family had to overcome to see that justice was properly dispensed far away from home, in another country, with an entirely different set of criminal procedural rules and laws, was difficult to navigate.

As I was my friend's attorney at the time of his death, his family asked that I act as their "legal liaison" to the Jamaican Prosecutor's Office and to the Jamaican Police Department. I participated in multiple police interviews with my client's widow because she was the primary witness to his murder. As a former prosecuting attorney, I was also allowed by the Court, as a professional courtesy, to sit at the prosecutor's table to consult with the prosecuting attorney during trial. What I observed about the Jamaican trial process from a front row seat was compelling enough to cause me to seriously consider educating the "world" regarding what to expect and how to act appropriately when faced with legal issues while traveling abroad.

One of the realities in life is that, regardless of what country you are in, it is never a pleasant experience to run afoul of the law and be forced to accept that someone else will be making a decision about your pecuniary, proprietary, or penal interests (your money, your property, or your freedom).

It is important to know what the laws are, how they apply to you, and how to navigate the legal system if you are charged with a crime. It is also very helpful to know what resources are available to you if you are the victim of a criminal act. At the end of the day, an "ounce of prevention is worth a pound of cure," so the more knowledge you have, the more ammunition you possess, and the more likely you will have a positive outcome.

If you are traveling to the Dominican Republic, the first thing you should pack is a copy of this book! The helpful information and tips contained in this volume will provide a great starting point for knowing what to do (and not to do!) when you arrive at your destination and will help ensure that you have a wonderful vacation or business trip unmarred by tangles with the law.

TABLE OF CONTENTS

Introduction 11

CHAPTER 1: About the Dominican Republic 19

CHAPTER 2: Customs 33

CHAPTER 3: Crime in The Dominican Republic. 41

CHAPTER 4: Criminal Law Violations. 49

CHAPTER 5: Alcohol-Related Offenses. 59

CHAPTER 6: Firearm & Ammunition Offenses 67

CHAPTER 7: Prostitution 75

CHAPTER 8: LGBTQ 87

CHAPTER 9: Sexually Motivated/Violent Crimes 97

CHAPTER 10: Arrested in the Dominican Republic 105

CHAPTER 11: Jails vs. Prisons: Conditions & Culture 119

CHAPTER 12: Helping a Friend or Relative Imprisoned in the
Dominican Republic. 127

CHAPTER 13: The Administration of Justice. 135

CHAPTER 14: Crime Victim Assistance. 143

CHAPTER 15: Police. 153

CHAPTER 16: How to Get Legal Help in the Dominican Republic 161

CHAPTER 17: Medical Facilities & Hospitals 167

CHAPTER 18: Driving in the Dominican Republic 175

CHAPTER 19: Nude Beaches & Clothing-Optional Resorts..........183

CHAPTER 20: Unusual Laws....................................189

CHAPTER 21: Traveling Safely 195

CHAPTER 22: Tourist Taxation................................ 203

CHAPTER 23: Long-Term Stays 209

CHAPTER 24: Civil Litigation 221

CHAPTER 25: Other Things to Know 233

CHAPTER 26: Quick Reference Guide 241

Emergency/Important Contact Numbers in the
Dominican Republic 253

Useful SPANISH Phrases.....................................255

Glossary 257

Acknowledgments...261

About the Author 263

INTRODUCTION

IN THIS CHAPTER

- About This Book
- Hypotheticals Used Throughout This Book
- How This Book is Organized
- Icons Used in This Book
- Where to Go From Here

INTRODUCTION

As a practicing attorney for over 34 years, I have encountered numerous clients who travel often, but are unaware of the laws of the land they are traveling to.

Therefore, many years ago, I decided to write a series of books that would explain the laws of specific countries. My focus was to explain the laws that may affect travelers in a straightforward manner, without all of the legal language that is sometimes hard for even seasoned attorneys to understand.

About This Book

The aim of this book is simple. It provides you, the traveler, with a simple, easy to read book that will provide a basic legal guide that explains the law in the country that you are about to visit. It is not intended to educate you on ALL of the laws in a given country. The goal is to provide you with the details of the most common legal and safety issues faced by tourists and business travelers.

I have also provided context with background information on places not to visit, statistics on the country and prevention measures you should take to safeguard your legal and physical safety. Knowledge is a powerful thing and knowing how to stay out of trouble (or how to get out of it!) is important for everyone who travels.

This *Law of The Land/Dominican Republic* book simply helps you become more informed about your legal rights, responsibilities, and obligations in a wide range of subject areas.

Last, but not least, this book does NOT purport to offer legal advice. It does, however, provide the information you need to stay safe, follow the law and navigate around legal difficulties. However, if you do face legal difficulties, the information in this book will provide you with a starting point for solving the problem and obtaining legal assistance should it be required.

Hypotheticals Used Throughout This Book

From time to time throughout this book, I will explain the law to readers by using hypothetical scenarios. These hypotheticals will be marked by an icon that will be explained in further detail as you read on.

How This Book is Organized

CHAPTER 1: **About the Dominican Republic.** This chapter will provide you with a brief overview about the Dominican Republic and its history. It also addresses Visa requirements, monetary advice, and the best times to visit.

CHAPTER 2: **Customs.** This chapter will provide information on what to expect when entering the Dominican Republic. It will also explain what restricted and prohibited items are when entering the Dominican Republic along with custom's regulations.

CHAPTER 3: **Crime in the Dominican Republic.** This chapter provides an overview of the history of crime in the Dominican Republic and steps that the Dominican Republic's officials have taken to curb the high rate of crime.

CHAPTER 4: **Criminal Law Violations.** This chapter will provide information on drug offenses, penalties, true events and questions and answers.

CHAPTER 5: **Alcohol-Related Offenses.** This chapter will provide key points regarding the sale, consumption, and regulations of alcohol use in the Dominican Republic.

CHAPTER 6: **Firearm & Ammunition Offenses.** This chapter will provide key points regarding the possession of firearms and ammunition in the Dominican Republic.

CHAPTER 7: **Prostitution.** This chapter provides an overview of the history of prostitution in the Dominican Republic, laws and penalties, prostitution practices, sex trafficking, sex tourism, health in the Dominican Republic, tips to avoid being hassled, a Law of the Land Hypothetical, and the current situation on prostitution in the Dominican Republic.

CHAPTER 8: **LGBTQ.** This chapter will provide information regarding the acceptance of LGBTQ people in the Dominican Republic and the laws surrounding homosexuality.

CHAPTER 9: **Sexually Motivated/Violent Crimes.** This chapter will provide an overview of sexually related crimes in the Dominican Republic.

CHAPTER 10: **Arrested in the Dominican Republic.** This chapter will provide information on what to do if you are arrested in the Dominican Republic.

CHAPTER 11: **Jails vs. Prisons: Conditions & Culture.** This chapter will provide information on the conditions and culture of the Dominican Republic's Jails and Prisons.

CHAPTER 12: **Helping a Friend or Relative Imprisoned in the Dominican Republic.** This chapter will provide information on how you can assist a friend or relative imprisoned in the Dominican Republic.

CHAPTER 13: **The Administration of Justice.** This chapter will provide information on the Dominican Republic's Legal System.

CHAPTER 14: Crime Victim Assistance. This chapter will provide information on crime victim assistance along with providing safety tips.

CHAPTER 15: Police. This chapter will provide information on the Dominican Republic's Police and how to report a crime.

CHAPTER 16: How to Get Legal Help in the Dominican Republic. This chapter will provide information regarding how to obtain legal assistance for travelers to the Dominican Republic.

CHAPTER 17: Medical Facilities & Hospitals. This chapter will provide information about how to obtain medical care while visiting the Dominican Republic.

CHAPTER 18: Driving in the Dominican Republic. This chapter will provide information on driving in the Dominican Republic, it's traffic rules, and road safety tips.

CHAPTER 19: Nude Beaches & Clothing-Optional Resorts. This chapter will provide an overview of nude beaches and clothing-optional resorts in the Dominican Republic, and the legality and safety of visiting nude beaches in the Dominican Republic.

CHAPTER 20: Unusual Laws. This chapter will provide information on some Unusual Laws in the Dominican Republic, and penalties and fines.

CHAPTER 21: Traveling Safely. This chapter will provide information on women traveling alone, crime prevention for families, safety notes for all travelers, and overall advice.

CHAPTER 22: Tourist Taxation. This chapter will provide information on taxes that tourists are required to pay in the Dominican Republic.

CHAPTER 23: Long-Term Stays. This chapter will provide an overview of the consequences for overstaying your visit to the Dominican Republic.

CHAPTER 24: Civil Litigation. This chapter will provide information about the civil litigation process in the Dominican Republic.

CHAPTER 25: **Other Things to Know.** This chapter will provide information on the harassment of tourists, travel and safety, and other practical tips.

CHAPTER 26: **Quick Reference Guide.** This chapter is a quick way to get information. It is a condensed version of the chapters in this book.

Emergency/Important Contact Numbers in the Dominican Republic

Useful Dominican Spanish Phrases

Glossary

Icons Used in this Book

What do those pictures throughout the book mean? See below:

 WARNING: This icon flags information about things you should **avoid** while visiting the Dominican Republic. Heed the advice next to this icon to avoid legal perils.

 REMEMBER: This icon flags noteworthy information that you **shouldn't forget.**

 HELPFUL TIPS: This icon flags information that will help you when entering the Dominican Republic, relates to a legal situation, or refers to resources available while visiting the Dominican Republic.

 TECHNICAL INFORMATION: This icon flags technical aspects of the law. If you are faced with a legal problem, and you want to learn more about the law involved, this information can be helpful.

 **ADDITIONAL INFORMATION**: This icon points to the location of additional information available on the internet.

 **HYPOTHETICAL**: This icon points to hypothetical scenarios to illustrate possible legal problems and the outcome.

 **QUESTIONS**: This icon points to questions and answers throughout the book.

 **TRUE STORY**: This icon points to true events throughout the book.

Where to Go From Here

If you have a specific question about the law in the Dominican Republic as it relates to a particular area, just turn to the chapter that addresses that issue, or turn to the Quick Reference Guide. You can also read the book from cover to cover to obtain a more comprehensive understanding of Dominican Republic laws and resources available should you find yourself in a legal predicament while visiting.

 **Disclaimer:** While the recommendations in this book primarily address U.S. citizens, the information is relevant and applicable to citizens of any country.

ABOUT THE DOMINICAN REPUBLIC

IN THIS CHAPTER

- About the Dominican Republic
- The Dominican Republic, the Basics
- Dominican Hospitality

CHAPTER 1
ABOUT THE DOMINICAN REPUBLIC

About the Dominican Republic[1]

The Dominican Republic is located on the island of **Hispaniola**, which it shares with Haiti. Situated in the Caribbean Sea, it is part of the Greater Antilles, a group of islands that includes Cuba and Puerto Rico. The country lies to the **east of Cuba** and to the **south of Puerto Rico**, bordered by the **Atlantic Ocean** to the north and the **Caribbean Sea** to the south. Covering an area of approximately 48,671 square kilometers (18,792 square miles), the Dominican Republic is the **second-largest country in the Caribbean**, after Cuba. With a population of about **11 million people** as of 2023, it is the most populous nation in the Caribbean and the second-most populous in Latin America, behind Cuba.

The Dominican Republic is widely recognized for its **breathtaking beaches**, particularly in popular tourist destinations. Its natural beauty extends beyond its coastline, with mountains such as Pico Duarte, the highest peak in the Caribbean, and lush rainforests offering diverse ecosystems. The country is also known for its **vibrant culture**, which includes the internationally recognized music genres of **merengue** and **bachata**. Santo Domingo, the capital, is the oldest continuously

---

1   https://www.britannica.com/place/Dominican-Republic

inhabited European settlement in the Americas and is home to the historic Zona Colonial, a UNESCO World Heritage site. The Dominican Republic also has a deep passion for **baseball**, producing a significant number of Major League Baseball players, many of whom are stars in the sport.

The Dominican Republic's history dates back to the arrival of Christopher Columbus in 1492, when it became the **first permanent European colony** in the Americas. The island was divided between **Spain** and **France** in the 17th century, with the western part becoming **Haiti** in 1804. After a series of conflicts, the Dominican Republic declared its independence from Haiti on February 27, 1844. The 19th and 20th centuries were marked by political instability, including the dictatorship of Rafael Trujillo from 1930 to 1961, whose regime was infamous for violence and repression. After his assassination, the country transitioned to **democracy**, and today, the Dominican Republic has a growing economy, driven by **tourism, agriculture**, and **services**. It is one of the fastest-growing economies in the Caribbean and plays a significant role in regional culture and politics.

The Capital

The capital of the Dominican Republic, **Santo Domingo**, is located on the southern coast of the island of Hispaniola, along the Caribbean Santo Domingo Sea. It is not only the **largest city** in the country but also a **key cultural, political**, and **economic hub** of the nation. The city is renowned for its historical significance, particularly in the **Zona Colonial**, which boasts the oldest cathedral in the Americas (the Cathedral of Santa María la Menor) and the Alcázar de Colón, the former residence of Christopher Columbus' son. These landmarks reflect Santo Domingo's role as the heart of Spanish colonial power in the New World. In addition to its historical charm, Santo Domingo has evolved into a **modern metropolis**, with a bustling urban scene. It is home to **vibrant markets, modern shopping centers**, a **thriving arts scene**, and **an exciting nightlife**. The city also hosts various festivals and cultural events, showcasing its rich heritage and diverse population. Santo Domingo's economy is driven by commerce, manufacturing, and services, and it is a **key gateway for tourism** in the Caribbean region. Despite its modernization, the city retains a strong connection to its past, making it an exciting **blend of old-world charm** and **contemporary development.**

The People

The people of the Dominican Republic, known as **Dominicans**, have a rich cultural heritage shaped by indigenous, African, and European influences. The origins of the Dominican people can be traced back to **the Taíno,** the island's indigenous inhabitants, who developed advanced agricultural practices, fishing techniques, and a complex social structure long before European contact. In 1492, Christopher Columbus arrived on the island, leading to the **Spanish colonization** that would dramatically alter the course of Dominican history. The Spanish introduced European customs, language, and religion, while also bringing African slaves to work in the sugar plantations, which had a profound impact on the development of the population's mixed heritage.

The Dominican Republic's social fabric is characterized by a blend of these cultural influences. **Afro-Dominicans**, who make up a significant portion of the population, have their roots in the enslaved Africans who were brought to the island during the colonial period. Over time, the blending of African, Spanish, and indigenous Taíno traditions gave rise to a **unique cultural identity** that is reflected in the country's music, dance (notably merengue and bachata), food, and language.

Dominican society values **strong family ties** and a **sense of community**, with social interactions often centered around family gatherings and neighborhood celebrations. The concept of *"compadrazgo"* (godparenthood) is also an important cultural practice, signifying strong social bonds and a sense of mutual support. Dominicans are known for their warmth and hospitality, often placing a strong emphasis on personal relationships.

Language

The official language of the Dominican Republic is **Spanish**, spoken by the majority of the population. Dominican Spanish has **unique characteristics**, influenced by Taíno, African, and European Spanish roots.

The language is known for its **fast-paced, informal speech,** often dropping syllables or blending words, and features colloquial expressions or *"Dominicanismos."*

While **Spanish** dominates, the language also incorporates African influences, especially in music, food, and daily life. Some **Taíno** words remain, particularly in place names and references to nature. Additionally, **English** is increasingly spoken, especially in tourist areas and among younger generations, due to the country's growing ties with the U.S. Language is a **key part of Dominican identity,** reflecting the nation's diverse cultural heritage.

Religion[2]

The predominant religion in the Dominican Republic is **Christianity,** with **Catholicism** being the most widely practiced faith. Around 70-80 percent of the population identifies as Roman Catholic, a reflection of the country's colonial history under Spain. Catholicism plays a significant role in the cultural and social life of Dominicans, influencing holidays, family traditions, and community events. In recent decades, **Protestantism** has grown significantly, especially among Evangelical Christians, now representing about 15-20 percent of the population. This shift is due in part to missionary activities and the rise of Protestant churches in both urban and rural areas.

Although the Dominican Republic is a predominantly Christian nation, there are also smaller communities practicing **other religions,** including **Judaism, Islam,** and **Buddhism.** Additionally, **folk religious practices,** often blending elements of Catholicism with African and indigenous beliefs, are common, especially in rural areas.

Affordability

The Dominican Republic is generally considered **an affordable destination** for travelers, especially compared to other Caribbean islands

---

2   https://www.iclrs.org/blurb/religion-in-the-dominican-republic/

or Latin American countries. The cost of travel can vary depending on where you stay, how you travel, and the activities you choose.

Accommodation options are diverse, ranging from budget-friendly hostels and guesthouses to luxury resorts. All-inclusive resorts are particularly popular and often provide good value, especially if you plan to stay within the resort. In urban areas like Santo Domingo or Santiago, you'll find reasonably priced hotels. When it comes to **food**, local cuisine is very affordable. Street food and small local eateries, known as "*comedor*," offer meals for just a few dollars. Dining in tourist areas or at upscale restaurants will cost more, but overall, meals are typically much cheaper than in many Western countries.

Transportation is also relatively cheap, with public transport like *guaguas* (buses) and *motoconchos* (motorcycle taxis) being inexpensive. Renting a car or using private taxis can be more expensive, especially in tourist-heavy areas. However, rideshare services like Uber are available in some cities and can offer a more affordable way to get around. As for **activities**, many of the country's attractions, such as beaches, hiking, and natural parks, are free or low-cost. Guided tours to popular sites like those in Santo Domingo or Punta Cana, along with excursions such as whale watching or historical tours, can add to your expenses.

The Dominican Republic, the Basics

How to Get There?

The Dominican Republic is a popular destination with a **number of major airports**, the largest of which include:

1. **Punta Cana International Airport** (**PUJ**): Located in the eastern part of the country, it is the busiest airport, handling the majority of international flights, especially from North America and Europe. It is a major hub for tourists heading to the popular Punta Cana resorts.

2. **Las Américas International Airport (SDQ)**: Situated near Santo Domingo, the capital city, SDQ is the second-busiest airport. It serves a large number of international flights, particularly to and from the U.S. and Latin America.

3. **Cibao International Airport (STI)**: Located in Santiago, this airport serves the northern region of the country. It handles a significant number of flights, particularly to the U.S. and Caribbean.

4. **La Romana International Airport (LRM)**: This airport is smaller but still significant for tourists, especially those visiting the luxury resorts in the La Romana area.

The Dominican Republic is served by a **variety of airlines** offering direct flights from North America and Europe, including:

- **American Airlines:** Offers numerous flights from the U.S. to Punta Cana, Santo Domingo, and other airports in the country.
- **JetBlue Airways:** A major carrier for flights between the U.S. and the Dominican Republic, including routes to Santo Domingo, Punta Cana, and Santiago.
- **Delta Airlines:** Serves many routes from the U.S. to the Dominican Republic, especially to Punta Cana and Santo Domingo.
- **United Airlines:** Provides flights to several Dominican airports, including Punta Cana and Santo Domingo.
- **Air France:** Operates flights from Paris to both Punta Cana and Santo Domingo.
- **Iberia:** Provides flights from Madrid to the Dominican Republic, primarily to Santo Domingo and Punta Cana.
- **Caribbean Airlines:** A regional carrier offering flights to various destinations within the Caribbean, including the Dominican Republic.

When to Visit?

The Dominican Republic offers something for every traveler, but the best time to visit depends on your priorities—whether it's ideal weather, avoiding crowds, or enjoying specific activities.

Weather-wise, the most pleasant weather occurs during the dry season from **December to April**, with warm temperatures, minimal rainfall, and sunny days perfect for outdoor activities. This is the peak season, so expect higher prices. The **off-season** from **May to November** is the rainy season, with June to November being the peak of hurricane season. While still warm, this time is less crowded and more affordable, though you may experience occasional rain.

Crowd-wise, the **peak season** from **December to April** sees more tourists and higher prices, especially during holidays like Christmas and Spring Break. The **off-season** offers fewer tourists and better deals, making it a great time for a more relaxed visit, though be mindful of the potential for rain.

Activities-wise, the dry season (December to April) is ideal for beach activities, while the windier months (November to April) are best for water sports like surfing and kiteboarding. The lush, green landscape from May to November is perfect for hiking and ecotourism, though occasional rain is expected.

For **festivals**, the best time to visit is during **Carnival** (February), celebrated with vibrant parades and traditional dances in cities like Santo Domingo and La Vega. The **Merengue Festival** (July) showcases the country's music and dance, while **Semana Santa** (Holy Week) in March or April features religious ceremonies and family events. Other notable events include **Dominican Independence Day** (February 27) and the **Dominican Republic Jazz Festival** (October/November).

 **Do I Need a Visa?**

Whether you need a visa to visit the Dominican Republic **depends on your nationality** and **the purpose of your trip**. For most tourists from countries like the **United States, Canada**, and the **European Union**, a visa is not required for stays of up to 30 days. However, visitors will need a **tourist card**, which can be purchased either at the airport upon arrival or online in advance. The cost of the tourist card is typically around **US$10.**

For travelers from **other countries,** a visa **may be required** before arrival. In these cases, it's important to check with the nearest Dominican embassy or consulate to confirm the specific visa requirements based on your nationality. If you plan to stay longer than 30 days, you can extend your stay for an additional 30 days by paying a fee at the Dominican Republic's Immigration Office.

If you're visiting for purposes **other than tourism,** such as business or study, you may need to apply for **a visa,** even if your country typically doesn't require one for short-term visits. It's always best to verify the latest entry requirements to ensure you have the necessary documentation for your trip.

How to Get Around

Getting around the Dominican Republic is fairly easy, with several convenient options for tourists. In popular tourist areas like Punta Cana and Santo Domingo, **taxis** and **Uber** are widely available and reliable. Uber, in particular, is a safe and affordable alternative to traditional taxis. For traveling between cities or exploring further regions, **buses** (*guaguas*) are an affordable option, although they can be crowded and less frequent. **Renting a car** offers the most flexibility, especially for those wanting to explore beyond major cities, though driving in busy urban areas can be challenging.

For short trips within cities, *motoconchos* (motorcycle taxis) are quick and inexpensive, but it's best to agree on a fare before getting on. If you're looking for a more unique way to explore, **jeep safaris** or **ATV tours** provide exciting opportunities to discover the countryside, beaches, and hidden gems with a guide. Depending on your itinerary and comfort level, taxis, Uber, and car rentals are the most convenient ways to get around for most tourists.

 **Monetary Advice**

The official currency of the Dominican Republic is the **Dominican Peso** (**DOP or RD$**). The exchange rate fluctuates, but typically, **US$1** is equivalent to around **RD$55-60**, though it can vary depending on the market. **Currency exchange** can be done at **banks, exchange bureaus,** and **ATMs** throughout the country, with ATMs generally offering the best rates. Major airports and tourist areas also have exchange services, but they may charge higher fees.

Credit cards are widely accepted in **tourist areas, hotels, restaurants,** and **larger shops** in the Dominican Republic. **Visa** and **Mastercard** are the most commonly accepted, while **American Express** isn't accepted as often, particularly outside major cities. It's always a good idea to carry **cash** for small purchases, street vendors, or in rural areas where credit card facilities may not be available. When using credit cards, be mindful of potential **foreign transaction fees**, which some banks or card providers may charge. It's also recommended to inform your bank ahead of time about your travel plans to avoid any issues with card usage abroad.

While the **U.S. dollar** (**USD**) is not the official currency, it is often accepted in many tourist spots, especially in **Punta Cana** and **Santo Domingo**. However, you may receive change in Dominican Pesos, so it's important to be aware of the exchange rate when paying in dollars.

In the Dominican Republic, **bargaining is common**, especially in local markets, street vendors, and tourist areas. While prices in fixed-price stores and restaurants are generally non-negotiable, you can often haggle in **informal settings**. The process is typically friendly and light-hearted, but if you're not comfortable negotiating, it's fine to accept the listed price. Be mindful that prices can be inflated in tourist-heavy spots, so knowing the average cost of goods or services can help avoid overpaying.

Similarly, **tipping** is widely practiced, and it's appreciated for good service. In **restaurants**, a tip of **10-15 percent** is standard, although many places already include a service charge. For **hotel staff**, tipping **US$1-2**

per day for housekeepers and **US$2-5 for bellhops** is common. **Taxi drivers** and **tour guides** typically receive a tip of **10-15 percent** of the fare or US$5-10, while motoconchos (motorcycle taxis) usually don't expect a tip, but rounding up the fare is a nice gesture. It's recommended to carry small bills in Dominican Pesos (DOP) for tipping, though U.S. dollars are widely accepted in tourist areas.

Dominican Hospitality

Dominican hospitality is centered around a **warm** and **welcoming attitude**, with an emphasis on friendliness, openness, and making guests feel like family. The Dominican Republic is known for its **friendly locals**, who often go out of their way to ensure that visitors feel at home. The country's culture of hospitality is rooted in its **strong sense of community**, where sharing and helping one another are highly valued. Visitors are often greeted with a smile and a hearty "¡Bienvenido!" (Welcome), and it's common to be invited to join locals for meals or celebrations.

Hospitality in the Dominican Republic is expressed through **genuine gestures of kindness**. It's not unusual for a local to offer a visitor a **refreshing drink**, a **handshake**, or even a **ride** to their destination if they need help. In rural areas, guests may be offered a **cup of coffee** or local treats like *mangu* (mashed plantains) as a sign of hospitality. Dominicans are often eager to share their **culture**, whether it's through music, dance, or simply offering advice and directions to travelers.

In the Dominican Republic, **politeness** is also highly valued, and showing respect is key to good relationships. While the Dominican approach to hospitality may not involve formal rituals, the essence of making someone feel comfortable and cared for is very much present. **Bowing or greeting with a handshake** is common and **making eye contact** when speaking is important for showing respect. Also, being **punctual** is valued, especially in business or formal settings, but there is generally a laid-back attitude toward time in social situations. **Respecting personal space**, such as addressing people by their titles or using polite language when speaking, is also a sign of good manners. Dominicans also take great pride in sharing their **food,** especially during social events or family gatherings, as food is a big part of their culture.

For visitors, showing appreciation through simple phrases like *"gracias"* (thank you) or *"muchas gracias"* (thank you very much) will be well-received. Engaging with locals in a friendly and respectful manner, especially by showing interest in their culture and traditions, will enhance the hospitality experience.

CHAPTER 2

CUSTOMS

IN THIS CHAPTER

- Travelers Entering the Dominican Republic
- Customs Entitlements and Monetary Restrictions
- Restricted and Prohibited Items
- Five Practical Tips to Know Before You Go

CHAPTER 2

CUSTOMS

Travelers Entering the Dominican Republic[3]

When traveling to the Dominican Republic, visitors are required to have a **valid passport** with **at least six months of validity** beyond the intended departure date. Most travelers will also need to purchase a **tourist card**, which costs around **US$10**. This card can be obtained upon arrival at the airport or in advance online. Additionally, travelers should be prepared to show proof of a **return or onward ticket** and, in some cases, a **visa**, depending on their nationality. While many countries, such as the U.S., Canada, and EU nations, do not require a visa for short stays, some visitors may need to obtain one before their trip. Health requirements may vary, depending on the current global health situation. It's always advisable to check for the **latest health-related entry requirements** before traveling.

Upon landing, travelers will go through the **standard immigration** process, where they will present their passport and tourist card (if applicable). Immigration officers may ask a few questions about the purpose of your visit, so it's important to have your travel details handy. After immigration, you will proceed to **customs**, where you may need to declare any items exceeding the allowed limits or answer questions regarding what you're bringing into the country. Depending on the current regulations, there may also be a **health screening**, although these are generally

---

3   https://www.godominicanrepublic.com/travel/entry-requirements/

not frequent anymore. Once cleared through immigration and customs, you'll head to **baggage claim** to pick up your luggage. Depending on the airport, this could be a quick process, though major airports like Punta Cana might have longer lines due to the large volume of tourists.

After collecting your baggage, you'll find various services, including **tourist information**, **currency exchange**, and **transportation options** like taxis or shuttles. While taxis are readily available, it's always a good idea to agree on a fare before starting the journey, or to use apps like **Uber** if available, which can provide a more predictable price.

It's important to keep your **tourist card** and **passport** safe, as the tourist card will need to be presented when you leave the country. Though the Dominican Republic is generally safe for tourists, it's always wise to stay alert in busy areas, particularly in airports or crowded markets. When choosing transportation, be cautious of inflated taxi prices at the airport; agreeing on the fare beforehand or opting for Uber can help you avoid surprises.

While many people in tourist areas speak some **English**, especially in larger cities or resorts, **Spanish** is the official language. Learning a few basic phrases, like *"hola"* (hello) and *"gracias"* (thank you), can go a long way in enhancing your experience.

 For the most up-to-date information, including travel advisories and health-related guidance, you can visit the **U.S. Department of State's Travel Advisory** website at **travel.state.gov**. Additionally, the **Dominican Republic Ministry of Tourism** website **godominicanrepublic.com** provides helpful travel tips, safety updates, and important information for visitors.

Customs Entitlements and Monetary Restrictions

When entering the Dominican Republic, there are specific customs entitlements and monetary restrictions that travelers should be aware of. Here are the key points on what you can and cannot bring into the country:

Currency:

The Dominican Republic does not impose a restriction on the amount of foreign currency (including U.S. dollars, euros, or other currencies) you can bring into the country. However, if you are carrying over **US$10,000** (or its equivalent in another currency), or **RD$100,000**, you must **declare** it to customs upon arrival. This is part of the country's efforts to prevent money laundering. Failure to declare amounts over these limits may result in penalties, including the confiscation of undeclared funds.

Permitted Items:

- **Personal Items:** Personal belongings such as clothes, toiletries, and electronics (phones, laptops, cameras) are permitted for personal use. There is no restriction on common items like books, magazines, or other personal comfort items.
- **Duty-Free Goods:** You can bring in duty-free items within the following limits:
    - **Alcohol:** Up to **1 liter of liquor** or **2 bottles of wine**.
    - **Tobacco:** Up to 200 cigarettes or 50 cigars.
    - **Perfume:** Reasonable amounts for personal use (typically around 50 mL).
- **Gifts and Souvenirs:** Gifts and souvenirs are allowed, provided they are for personal use and not for resale. However, if you bring excessive quantities, particularly of items like electronics or clothing, customs may inspect them further to ensure they are not for commercial use.
- **Food:** Food items for personal use are generally permitted, but there are restrictions on certain products. Processed and packaged snacks or candies are typically allowed, while fresh fruits, meats, dairy products, and items that may pose a biosecurity risk (like plant-based

products) are either restricted or require inspection. Always verify if any specific food items you plan to bring are on the restricted list.

- **Medicines:** You are allowed to bring prescription medications for personal use, but they must comply with Dominican Republic's regulations. Certain over-the-counter medications available in other countries may be restricted. It's a good idea to bring a doctor's prescription or note if you're carrying prescription medication, especially if it contains controlled substances, such as narcotics or certain stimulants, which are prohibited.

- **Electronics:** Personal electronics such as smartphones, laptops, cameras, and other devices are allowed for personal use. However, bringing in large quantities of electronics may raise questions about whether they are for resale. It's recommended to limit the number of high-value electronics you bring to avoid potential customs scrutiny.

- **Cosmetics and Toiletries:** Small amounts of cosmetics and toiletries for personal use are allowed. However, large quantities, like bulk purchases of lotions, perfumes, or other beauty products, could be questioned by customs. Keep personal-use items in their original packaging to avoid complications.

By following these guidelines, you'll help ensure a smooth customs process when entering the Dominican Republic. Always declare any large sums of money and be mindful of prohibited or restricted items to avoid complications.

 ## Restricted and Prohibited Items

The country has specific rules regarding prohibited and restricted items, which include certain goods, currency limits, and agricultural products that may pose risks to local ecosystems. Familiarizing yourself with these guidelines will help you avoid complications at customs and ensure that you comply with local laws. For example, **illegal drugs and narcotics** of any kind, including marijuana, are **strictly prohibited**. Even small amounts can result in severe penalties, including fines, arrest, and imprisonment. The same applies to **firearms, ammunition**, and **explosives**; these are generally banned unless you have a special permit, and other weapons are not allowed either.

Another category that travelers need to be aware of is **counterfeit goods**. Fake items, such as clothing, shoes, handbags, electronics, and accessories, are not permitted. If caught with counterfeit products, customs officers will confiscate them, and you could face legal consequences. Similarly, the import of **endangered species products** is prohibited. This includes items made from animals like ivory, certain types of leather, and animal skins, which are not allowed into the country. Products such as jewelry, handbags, shoes, and clothing made from these materials fall under this restriction.

The import of **pornographic material** is also banned, and any such items found in your possession could be seized. You should also be mindful of **fresh fruits, vegetables, and plants**. These items are restricted due to the potential risk they pose to local agriculture by carrying pests and diseases. Some plant products may require special permits to be imported. Along with these restrictions, **unlicensed pharmaceuticals** are prohibited as well. Some over-the-counter medications that are legal in other countries may be banned in the Dominican Republic, so it's always best to check ahead if you're carrying any medications.

There are also **restricted items** that you can bring into the country under certain conditions. For example, **agricultural products** like fresh food, meats, and dairy may be subject to inspection or outright prohibition, and some may require a permit for entry. If you're traveling with **pets**, such as dogs or cats, they can be imported, but they need to meet health certification requirements, including vaccinations like rabies. Exotic animals and wildlife are subject to additional restrictions.

As for **medicines**, while prescription medications for personal use are generally allowed, some may be restricted, and you may need to provide documentation, especially for those containing controlled substances. Cultural artifacts and antiquities, which are part of the Dominican Republic's heritage, may also be restricted from export or import. Finally, while travelers can bring a reasonable amount of **alcohol and tobacco** for personal use, excessive quantities may be subject to customs duties.

Similarly, large quantities of **electronics** could raise suspicions that they are intended for resale, so customs may flag them for inspection.

Five Practical Tips to Know Before You Go

1. Though many people speak English in tourist areas, knowing a few Spanish phrases like *"Hola"* (Hello) and *"Gracias"* (Thank you) will be appreciated and help you connect with locals.

2. Dominicans are known for their hospitality. A friendly *"¿Cómo está?"* (How are you?) or a smile goes a long way in making positive connections.

3. Sunday is family day, and many businesses may close early, especially in rural areas. Also, holidays like **Carnival** and **Semana Santa** are celebrated with festivities, but businesses may be closed.

4. It's customary to leave a **10 percent tip** at restaurants. Hotel staff, taxi drivers, and tour guides also appreciate tips for good service.

5. While beachwear is fine at the beach, it's best to wear more modest clothing when visiting churches, historical sites, or rural areas out of respect for local customs.

CRIME IN THE DOMINICAN REPUBLIC

IN THIS CHAPTER

- Overview
- Crime Hotspots in the Dominican Republic
- Crime Statistics
- Quick Safety Tips

CHAPTER 3

CRIME IN THE DOMINICAN REPUBLIC

Overview

The Dominican Republic is considered to be **relatively safe** for tourists, especially in major tourist destinations, resorts, and urban centers. Most visitors experience little to no criminal activity during their stay. However, like many countries, there are areas where crime is more prevalent, particularly in **poorer neighborhoods** or areas with fewer tourists. While the country isn't considered to be particularly dangerous, travelers should still exercise caution, especially in isolated or less-patrolled areas.

Several factors contribute to crime in the Dominican Republic. **Economic inequality** plays a significant role, as poverty and high unemployment rates in certain regions can drive petty crimes such as theft and pickpocketing. Additionally, the country's **proximity to major drug-producing regions** has made it a significant transit point for narcotics, which can lead to organized crime and drug-related violence. In tourist-heavy areas, the presence of **large numbers of visitors** can attract criminals involved in petty crimes like scams, thefts, and pickpocketing. In some urban areas, gang activity and turf wars contribute to localized violence. Moreover, issues like **corruption** and **inconsistent enforcement of laws** in certain regions further complicate efforts to combat crime.

In terms of crime trends, recent years have shown a **gradual decline** in certain types of crime. **Violent crime**, such as homicides and armed robberies, has remained relatively **stable over time**, with occasional upticks in specific areas due to gang-related violence or drug trafficking. However, these incidents typically do not affect tourists directly. **Petty crime**, including pickpocketing and theft, remains a consistent issue, but it is mostly confined to tourist areas and tends not to show significant increases. **Drug-related crimes** continue to be a **concern in some regions**, largely due to the country's role in the international drug trade. While the Dominican Republic has made efforts to crack down on drug trafficking and gang-related violence, these problems are more likely to affect local communities rather than international visitors.

Crime Hotspots in the Dominican Republic

Crime in the Dominican Republic tends to be concentrated in certain areas, particularly in **urban** and **economically disadvantaged regions**. **Santo Domingo**, the capital, has neighborhoods with higher crime rates, such as **Villa Consuelo**, **La Ciénaga**, and **Los Guandules**. These areas are known for petty theft, robberies, and occasional violent crime, driven largely by poverty and gang activity. While tourist zones like the Zona Colonial are generally safe, it's important to exercise caution when venturing into less populated or lower-income neighborhoods. In **Santiago**, the second-largest city, areas such as **Cienfuegos** and parts of **Los Salados** have higher crime rates, with incidents of petty crime and, in some cases, violent crime. While this is not a major issue for tourists, it's advisable to stay alert in these areas.

Tourist destinations such as **Puerto Plata**, **Cabarete**, and **Sosúa** also report some incidents of theft and scams, particularly in less-patrolled, isolated areas. Sosúa, which is popular for its nightlife, has seen occasional robberies and violence, mostly during the late hours or in less frequented parts. In **La Romana** and **Boca Chica**, both popular for their beaches and resorts, there are occasional reports of theft and assault, but these incidents typically happen outside of main resort areas or in less-policed zones. Rural areas like **Hato Mayor**, which are less frequented by tourists, can also see higher instances of robbery and violent crime, though these regions are not typical destinations for travelers.

When comparing crime rates, the Dominican Republic has similar issues with petty crime to countries like Mexico and Jamaica, with incidents of **theft**, **pickpocketing**, and **occasional violent crime**. However, when compared to major U.S. cities, the Dominican Republic generally has lower rates of violent crime, although petty crime such as theft is more common in tourist areas. Cities like New York, Los Angeles, and Chicago also experience incidents of theft and violent crime, though they tend to have higher overall crime rates.

 Before traveling, it's always a good idea to check **official travel advisories** from your home country. For example, the U.S. Department of State provides up-to-date travel warnings and safety information for the Dominican Republic on their website at **travel.state.gov/content/travel/en/traveladvisories/traveladvisories/dominican-republic-travel-advisory.html**. These advisories offer insights into safety concerns, including crime trends and areas of caution, and provide valuable information to ensure a safer trip. Always stay informed about the current situation to make informed decisions about where to go and how to stay safe while traveling.

Crime Statistics

Crime in the Dominican Republic is generally divided into two main categories: **petty crimes** and **violent crimes**. Petty crimes like **pickpocketing**, **theft**, and **scams** are the most common and widespread, particularly in **tourist areas**, **beach resorts**, and **bustling urban centers**. These crimes are typically opportunistic and target tourists who may be less familiar with the local environment. On the other hand, **violent crimes** such as **robbery**, **assault**, and, in some cases, **homicide**, while less frequent, still occur in certain neighborhoods, especially in **high-crime areas** or in regions with gang activity.

The most common crimes impacting tourists are related to **petty theft**. Visitors, especially in busy tourist zones, may find themselves targeted by thieves who engage in **pickpocketing** or **bag-snatching**. **Scams** are also prevalent, with tourists sometimes being tricked by dishonest vendors or taxi drivers who overcharge or deceive them about prices. In certain areas, tourists may also be at risk for **robberies**, particularly if traveling alone or at night in poorly lit or less-populated areas. **Violent crimes** like **assaults** or **sexual violence** against tourists are less common but do occasionally occur, particularly in areas known for nightlife or where tourists may be more vulnerable after drinking.

In terms of **global comparisons**, the Dominican Republic's **crime rate tends to be higher** than that of many developed countries, especially in categories of **petty crime**. In comparison to **regional averages**, the country fares similarly to **Mexico** and **Jamaica**, which experience higher instances of petty crime, especially in urban and tourist zones. Violent crime in the Dominican Republic is generally lower than in countries with higher levels of gang violence or political instability, such as **Honduras** or **El Salvador**, but still more common than in Western European countries.

As for **law enforcement**, there are ongoing concerns about its effectiveness. **Corruption** within the police force is a significant issue in some parts of the country, which has contributed to the perception that law enforcement can be inconsistent and unreliable. While efforts have been made in recent years to improve police presence in tourist areas, the issue of police corruption often undermines the ability to address crime at the grassroots level. In some cases, victims of crime may feel that police responses are delayed or ineffective. However, larger cities and tourist hotspots like **Punta Cana** or **Santo Domingo** have **police patrols** focused on maintaining safety in high-traffic areas, and many tourists report positive interactions with police in these regions.

 **Quick Safety Tips**

- Keep your belongings, such as wallets, phones, and jewelry, out of sight, especially in crowded areas.

- Always opt for official taxis or reputable ride-sharing apps like Uber to avoid unsafe or unlicensed drivers.

- Stick to well-lit, populated areas and avoid wandering in unfamiliar or poorly lit streets after dark.

- Choose well-known hotels or resorts with good security measures to ensure your safety.

- Watch out for overly friendly strangers, street vendors, or offers that seem too good to be true, especially in tourist-heavy areas.

- Lock doors and windows, use hotel safes for valuables, and always check that your room has adequate security features.

CRIMINAL LAW VIOLATIONS

IN THIS CHAPTER

- Marijuana and Other Drugs in the Dominican Republic
- Penalties
- Prescription Medication
- General Questions
- Law of the Land Hypothetical
- Takeaways

CRIMINAL LAW VIOLATIONS

Marijuana and Other Drugs in the Dominican Republic

Cannabis has a long, complex history in the Dominican Republic. In the past, marijuana use was relatively uncommon, but in recent decades, the plant has become more visible, especially in urban areas and among certain subcultures. Cannabis has **traditionally been illegal**, and the Dominican Republic has had **strict laws** surrounding its cultivation, distribution, and consumption. The country has a **long-standing prohibition on marijuana use**, dating back to the 20th century when the global War on Drugs shaped policies around drug use. In recent years, however, there has been growing debate about marijuana's potential medicinal benefits and its economic implications. Despite this, cannabis use remains largely criminalized, and law enforcement continues to arrest individuals for possession or use.

The Dominican Republic has made limited steps toward recognizing **medical marijuana**, but it has **not yet legalized or regulated** it on a **national level**. There have been discussions about the potential therapeutic benefits of cannabis, particularly for conditions such as chronic pain and epilepsy. However, legal access to medical marijuana is **not widely available**, and those seeking medical use of cannabis often resort to informal or illegal sources. **Recreational use** of marijuana **remains illegal** in the Dominican Republic. The country has strict drug laws, and cannabis is classified as a **controlled substance**. The penalties for possession, sale, or trafficking can be severe, including heavy fines and imprisonment. While cannabis is sometimes used in private settings or within certain communities, law enforcement actively patrols for violations, and tourists can face significant legal consequences if caught using or possessing marijuana.[4]

In the Dominican Republic, **synthetic cannabinoids** (often known as "Spice" or "K2") are **illegal**, and their use or possession is strictly prohibited. These substances are chemically engineered to mimic the effects of natural cannabis, but they can be far more potent and unpredictable, leading to dangerous health consequences. Synthetic cannabinoids are often sprayed onto plant material and smoked or vaporized, but their effects can be intense, including hallucinations, violent behavior, and even death. The Dominican government has made efforts to regulate and control the sale and use of synthetic drugs due to the severe health risks they pose. As a result, law enforcement is actively targeting the distribution and use of synthetic cannabinoids, treating them as dangerous substances under the country's drug laws. Those caught with synthetic cannabinoids face severe penalties similar to those for other illegal narcotics.

The laws concerning other drugs in the Dominican Republic are among the strictest in the Caribbean. Narcotics like **cocaine, heroin, methamphetamines**, and **ecstasy** are considered **illegal**, and their possession, distribution, or trafficking is met with harsh consequences. The legal framework is clear: possessing even a small amount of these substances can result in arrest and lengthy prison sentences, with convictions for trafficking or dealing large amounts of these drugs often leading to life imprisonment.

---

4   https://www.hopegrown.org/blog/traveling-with-medical-marijuana-is-it-legal-to-bring-it-to-the-dominican-republic

Penalties[5]

Penalties for drug-related offenses **vary** depending on the quantity of drugs involved. For **smaller amounts**, individuals may face **lighter sentences**, but **larger quantities** typically lead to much more severe consequences, including **imprisonment** for trafficking offenses. **Drug trafficking**, especially on an international scale, is a **serious crime** in the Dominican Republic, and law enforcement treats it with utmost rigor. Those involved in drug distribution, especially those caught manufacturing or transporting large amounts of illegal drugs, face **significant prison terms**. Drug-related offenses are also heavily penalized in terms of driving under the influence of drugs. A person caught driving while impaired by narcotics can face fines, license suspensions, or even imprisonment.

Given the Dominican Republic's geographic location, it is often used as a transit point for drug trafficking between South America and the United States. As a result, the government has made combating drug smuggling a priority, working in coordination with international partners to curb the flow of illegal substances. Law enforcement **regularly conducts patrols** and **raids targeting drug users and traffickers**, and police are vigilant in apprehending individuals who break the country's stringent drug laws. Even tourists are not immune to these laws; visitors caught possessing illegal drugs, including synthetic cannabinoids, **face harsh legal consequences**. The penalties for such offenses can include **arrest**, **detention**, or **imprisonment**, and foreign nationals can also **face deportation** or a **ban from re-entering the country**.

Prescription Medication[6]

When traveling to the Dominican Republic, it's important to understand the regulations surrounding prescription and over-the-counter

---

5   https://dr1.com/forums/threads/drug-laws-in-the-dr.113579/

6   https://www.tripadvisor.com/ShowTopic-g147293-i28-k1167135-o10-Taking_prescription_meds_to_the_DR-Punta_Cana_La_Altagracia_Province_Dominican_Republic.html

(OTC) medications. **Prescription medications** should always be kept in their **original packaging**, clearly labeled with your name, the dosage, and the prescribing doctor. It's essential to carry a **copy of the prescription**, ideally translated into **Spanish**, to avoid issues at customs. Some medications, especially those containing **controlled substances** like opioids or sedatives, may require additional documentation or approval to bring into the country. If you're unsure about whether a medication is allowed, it's advisable to consult the **Dominican Embassy** beforehand.

For **OTC medications**, common remedies like **pain relievers** or **cough syrups** are generally allowed in small quantities for personal use, but bringing large amounts, particularly those containing **pseudoephedrine**, could raise suspicion. It's best to bring only what you need and keep them in their original packaging.

The Dominican Republic has strict drug laws, and failing to declare medications or attempting to bring in unapproved substances can lead to **seizure of the drugs, fines**, or even **arrest**. Foreign visitors may also face deportation and be **banned from re-entering**. To avoid complications, **consult your doctor** and the **Dominican Embassy**, ensure you have the necessary documentation, and pack medications carefully. By following these guidelines, you can avoid legal issues and ensure your medications are properly handled during your stay.

 **General Questions**

1. *Is cannabis legal in the Dominican Republic?* **No.** Cannabis is illegal in the Dominican Republic. Both recreational and medicinal use of marijuana is prohibited, and possession or trafficking of cannabis can result in severe penalties, including imprisonment.

2. *Can I legally purchase marijuana in the Dominican Republic?* **No**. Marijuana cannot be legally purchased in the Dominican Republic. Cannabis remains a controlled substance, and there are no legal channels for purchasing marijuana in the country. Attempting to buy or possess marijuana can lead to significant legal consequences.

3. *Can I have marijuana on my person or in my hotel room in the Dominican Republic?* **No**. It is illegal to possess marijuana on your person or in a hotel room in the Dominican Republic. Possession of any amount of marijuana is prohibited, and if caught, you could face serious legal consequences, including arrest, fines, or imprisonment.

4. *Are there any other exceptions to the possession and consumption of cannabis in the Dominican Republic?* **No**. There are **no exceptions** for the possession or consumption of cannabis in the Dominican Republic. Marijuana remains illegal, both recreationally and medicinally, and there are no legal provisions for its use or possession.

5. *What are the penalties for possessing and consuming other types of illicit drugs in the Dominican Republic?* The penalties for possessing and consuming illicit drugs such as cocaine, heroin, methamphetamines, or synthetic cannabinoids in the Dominican Republic are severe. Depending on the quantity, offenders can face imprisonment, heavy fines, and, in some cases, life sentences for trafficking. Consumption or possession of even small amounts can lead to arrest, lengthy prison terms, or deportation for foreign nationals.

Law of the Land Hypothetical

HYPOTHETICAL: *John, a tourist from Canada, is planning a two-week vacation in the Dominican Republic. He uses medical marijuana to manage chronic back pain and has a prescription for CBD oil with minimal THC content. John has heard that marijuana laws in the Dominican Republic are strict, but he's unsure whether his CBD oil is allowed. Can John legally bring his CBD oil into the Dominican Republic, and what legal issues could arise from possessing marijuana-related products in the country?*

ANSWER: *John should be cautious about bringing CBD oil into the Dominican Republic. While CBD is legal in many countries, the Dominican Republic treats all marijuana-related products, including CBD oil, as controlled substances. Even though John has a medical marijuana prescription from Canada, the country does not recognize medical marijuana, and there are no clear regulations allowing the use of CBD products. If John tries to bring CBD oil, customs could confiscate it, and he risks facing fines, seizure, or even arrest. The best course of action is to leave the CBD oil at home, consult with the Dominican Embassy about the regulations, and consider alternative pain management options while in the country. This will help avoid potential legal complications during his trip.*

Takeaways

- Cannabis, including synthetic cannabinoids, remains illegal in the Dominican Republic. Despite ongoing debates about its medicinal use, marijuana is criminalized, and possession or trafficking can result in severe penalties, including imprisonment and fines.

- Drug-related offenses are heavily penalized, with harsher consequences for larger quantities. Trafficking or possessing significant amounts of drugs like cocaine or heroin can lead to long prison sentences, with life imprisonment for serious trafficking.

- Prescription medications should be in their original packaging with a copy of the prescription (ideally translated into Spanish). Controlled substances may require additional documentation. Failing to comply can lead to fines, seizure, or arrest.

- Dominican law enforcement actively polices drug use and trafficking. Tourists are not exempt from these laws and can face deportation or a ban from re-entering the country for violations.

- Visitors to the Dominican Republic must adhere to the country's strict drug laws. Tourists caught possessing illegal substances, including marijuana and synthetic drugs, can face arrest, deportation, or a ban from re-entering the country, regardless of their nationality.

ALCOHOL-RELATED OFFENSES

IN THIS CHAPTER

- Alcohol-Related Offenses
- Alcohol Regulation
- Things to Remember
- General Questions
- Law of the Land Hypothetical
- Takeaways

ALCOHOL-RELATED OFFENSES

Alcohol-Related Offenses

Alcohol is a staple in social life in the Dominican Republic. It is often consumed in **family gatherings**, **festivals**, and **public celebrations**. Dominican culture is centered around communal experiences, and alcohol plays a key part in these moments, helping to foster a sense of togetherness and relaxation. It is common to see people enjoying drinks during meals, barbecues, or beach outings. The consumption of alcohol is also frequent during **holidays** and **local fiestas**, including wedding celebrations, religious festivities, and traditional gatherings. In the daily life of Dominicans, alcohol is often a way to unwind, especially after a long day of work.

The Dominican Republic is best known for its rum, which has a strong cultural and historical presence in the country. The country is one of the **world's largest producers of rum**, and it is often considered the national spirit. Dominican rum is typically served **neat, on the rocks**, or as part of a **cocktail**. Some of the most popular drinks include:

- **Mamajuana:** A traditional Dominican drink made from rum, red wine, honey, and a mixture of local herbs and spices. It is often considered a **natural aphrodisiac**, is believed to have medicinal properties, and is commonly consumed in both social and ceremonial settings.

- **Rum-based Cocktails:** The **"Cuba Libre"** (rum, cola, and lime) and the **"Presidente"** (rum with fruit juices) are popular cocktails in the Dominican Republic, especially in tourist areas.

- **Presidente Beer:** Although rum is the dominant alcoholic drink, beer also plays a role in Dominican drinking culture. **Presidente** is the country's most famous beer and is widely consumed during outdoor activities or social events.

- **Santo Domingo Cocktails:** In more recent years, **local cocktails**, often featuring rum combined with tropical fruits like mango, passionfruit, or pineapple, have grown in popularity.

Alcohol is **legal** and **widely available** throughout the Dominican Republic. It is sold in supermarkets, bars, restaurants, and local markets, making it easily accessible for both locals and tourists. There are no significant legal restrictions on purchasing or consuming alcohol in public spaces, although drinking in certain areas may be regulated or restricted, such as near schools or religious institutions.

The **drinking age** is **18**, and while it is typically observed, enforcement may vary, especially in more remote areas. In major cities and tourist destinations like **Santo Domingo**, **Punta Cana**, and **Sosúa**, it's easy to find a variety of local and imported alcoholic beverages in both retail stores and bars.

Public consumption is **generally accepted**, especially in outdoor spaces, and **beachside bars** are a popular setting for enjoying cold drinks. In tourist areas, many bars and clubs stay open late, with alcohol readily available to patrons.

Alcohol Regulation[7]

In the Dominican Republic, **consuming alcohol in public places** such as streets, parks, and beaches is **strictly prohibited**. Drinking is allowed in designated areas like bars, restaurants, and private residences, but

---

7   https://jjstudiophoto.com/dominican-republic-drinking-laws

outside of these spaces, public drinking is considered illegal. This includes consuming alcohol in vehicles and on motorcycles, where it is also prohibited to transfer alcohol to the driver if the seal of the bottle has been broken. These regulations are designed to maintain public order and reduce the risk of accidents or disruptions caused by public intoxication.[8]

Alcohol sales are regulated with **specific hours**. From Monday to Saturday, alcohol can be sold between 8:00 a.m. and midnight, while on Sundays, sales begin at 12:00 p.m. and end at midnight. However, these hours may vary depending on location and local regulations, so it is advisable to check with local authorities or establishments to ensure compliance.

Alcohol advertising in the Dominican Republic is **subject to strict rules**. Advertisements for alcoholic beverages are only allowed on radio and television between 9:00 pm and 6:00 am. Additionally, all alcohol-related ads must include **mandatory health warnings**. These warnings include messages such as "It is prohibited to sell intoxicating beverages to minors" and "Excessive use of alcohol is harmful," in an effort to raise awareness about the risks associated with alcohol consumption.[9]

The **enforcement of drinking laws** is handled by both the National Police and the Ministry of Public Health. **The National Police** monitors establishments to ensure they are adhering to alcohol sale regulations and works to prevent underage drinking. They are also responsible for controlling public drinking in unauthorized areas. **The Ministry of Public Health** oversees the safety and quality of alcoholic beverages and enforces public health measures related to alcohol consumption. These agencies work together to ensure that the regulations are followed, and that alcohol consumption does not pose a threat to public safety or health.

---

8   https://movendi.ngo/news/2021/09/27/dominican-republic-law-passes-to-regulate-alcohol-sale-and-consumption/

9   https://iardwebprod.azurewebsites.net/science-resources/detail/Health-Warning-Labeling-Requirements

Penalties for violating drinking laws in the Dominican Republic can be significant. **Underage drinking** can lead to fines, mandatory alcohol education programs, or community service. **Public consumption** of alcohol may result in fines, confiscation of alcohol, or detention by authorities, as authorities work to ensure public order is maintained and discourage disruptive behaviors associated with excessive drinking. Individuals caught **driving under the influence** face fines, temporary suspension of their driver's license, or imprisonment. **The legal blood alcohol content (BAC) limit** is **0.05 percent**, and anyone caught exceeding this limit is subject to legal action. **Selling alcohol to minors** is a serious offense, with penalties including hefty fines, imprisonment, or revocation of business licenses.

Things to Remember

- **Drinking Age:** The legal drinking age in the Dominican Republic is **18 years old**. Both locals and tourists must adhere to this law.

- **ID:** You need a **valid ID** to purchase alcohol if you appear underage. Tourists often use their **passport** as identification, while locals may use a national ID card.

- **Public Consumption:** It is **illegal** to drink alcohol in public places such as streets, parks, and beaches. Public drinking is only allowed in designated areas like **bars, restaurants**, and **private residences**. Disruptive behavior due to alcohol consumption can result in penalties.

- **Public Drunkenness:** Public drunkenness can lead to **fines, alcohol confiscation**, or **detention** if the behavior causes disruptions. In extreme cases, more serious legal actions may follow.

- **Drunk Driving:** The **legal blood alcohol content (BAC) limit** for drivers is **0.05 percent**. Penalties for driving under the influence include **fines, license suspension**, or **imprisonment**. For severe cases or repeat offenses, harsher penalties can be imposed.

- **Purchase of Alcohol:** Alcohol can be purchased from **8:00 a.m. to midnight** Monday through Saturday, and from **12:00 p.m.**

to midnight on Sundays. However, you must be **18 years old** or older to purchase alcohol. Restrictions on sale hours may vary by location.

- **Alcohol Permits:** No special permits are required for **private events** like family gatherings or parties at home. However, **approval** is required for large **public gatherings** or events where alcohol is being served, especially in public spaces.

- **Illegal Alcohol:** While not a widespread issue, there are concerns about **counterfeit** alcohol or **illegally imported alcohol** in certain areas. It's advisable to buy alcohol from reputable, licensed outlets to avoid health risks associated with unregulated alcohol.

 **General Questions**

1. *Can I possess an open container in public?* **No.** In the Dominican Republic, it is **illegal** to possess or carry an open container of alcohol in public places such as streets, parks, beaches, or sidewalks. Alcohol consumption is restricted to **licensed establishments** and violating this law can result in fines, confiscation of alcohol, or other penalties.

2. *How does the enforcement of public drinking laws in the Dominican Republic affect tourists, and what steps can they take to ensure they are complying with local regulations?* The Dominican Republic enforces strict laws against public drinking, and tourists can face fines, alcohol confiscation, or detention if caught drinking in public spaces like streets, parks, or beaches. Public drunkenness, especially if disruptive, can also lead to penalties. To avoid issues, tourists should only consume alcohol in licensed venues such as bars, restaurants, or private residences, and be aware of the legal alcohol sale hours (8:00 a.m. to midnight, with a later start on Sundays). It's also important to drink responsibly, as excessive intoxication can lead to legal trouble.

 **Law of the Land Hypothetical**

HYPOTHETICAL: *Maria, a tourist in Santo Domingo, enjoys a few drinks at a local bar before heading back to her hotel by taxi. As she sips her drink in the backseat, the driver pulls over and informs her that consuming alcohol in the vehicle is prohibited. Is it illegal to drink alcohol in a taxi in the Dominican Republic?*

ANSWER: *Yes. It is illegal to consume alcohol in vehicles, including taxis, in the Dominican Republic. Even if the alcohol is sealed, transferring it to the driver or drinking in the passenger area is prohibited. Maria should finish her drink before getting into the vehicle to avoid any legal issues, as drinking in a car can lead to fines or other penalties.*

 **Takeaways**

- Public consumption of alcohol is prohibited in the Dominican Republic, including in public places like streets, parks, and beaches. Drinking is only permitted in licensed establishments or private properties.

- The legal drinking age in the country is **18**, and both locals and tourists must adhere to this law. Valid identification is required to purchase alcohol if an individual appears underage.

- The National Police and Ministry of Public Health are responsible for enforcing alcohol-related laws. Violations, such as underage drinking or public drunkenness, can result in fines, alcohol confiscation, or detention.

- The legal blood alcohol concentration (BAC) limit for drivers is **0.05 percent**. Those caught driving under the influence face fines, potential imprisonment, and suspension of their driver's license.

- The penalties for violating alcohol-related laws can be severe, including fines, imprisonment, and the revocation of business licenses for those selling alcohol to minors. Public drunkenness or disruptive behavior can lead to legal action and detention.

CHAPTER 6
FIREARM & AMMUNITION OFFENSES

IN THIS CHAPTER

- Current Firearm Status
- Legal Requirements for Purchasing, Carrying, and Using a Firearm
- Firearm Restrictions for Visitors
- Penalties
- General Questions
- Law of the Land True Story
- Takeaways

CHAPTER 6

FIREARM & AMMUNITION OFFENSES

Current Firearm Status

In the Dominican Republic, firearm ownership is **allowed but strictly regulated**. Only Dominican citizens and legal residents are permitted to own firearms, and even then, they must meet several criteria. Citizens must obtain a **permit** from the Ministry of the Interior and Police to own or carry a firearm, and the process includes background checks, psychological evaluations, and training requirements. Firearms are classified into different categories, with permits for concealed carry being more restrictive than for non-concealed weapons. The law also mandates **registration of firearms** and violations, such as carrying a weapon without proper authorization or involvement in illegal activities, can lead to severe penalties, including imprisonment. Despite these regulations, the country struggles with illegal firearms trafficking, leading to challenges in enforcement and public safety.

Legal Requirements for Purchasing, Carrying, and Using a Firearm

In the Dominican Republic, firearm ownership is tightly regulated to ensure public safety while allowing for personal defense and certain recreational activities. Individuals seeking to own a firearm must meet specific requirements and follow strict procedures, with regulations governing the types of firearms they can possess, how they must be stored, and where they are allowed to carry them.

Individuals must be **at least 21 years old**, and they must pass a thorough **background check**. This check includes ensuring that the individual has no criminal record, particularly for violent crimes, as such a record would disqualify them from ownership. Furthermore, the law requires individuals to be **mentally fit**, meaning that a medical evaluation is part of the application process. Applicants are also required to complete a firearm safety course to demonstrate that they understand how to safely handle and store weapons.[10]

Once all the prerequisites are met, an individual must seek **approval from the Ministry of the Interior and Police**, who will review the application and issue a firearm license if the conditions are fulfilled. This license is typically granted for a period of **two years**, and its renewal requires undergoing additional background checks and medical assessments.

While civilians are allowed to own firearms, the types of weapons they can possess are regulated. **Handguns** are the most common firearm for personal use, and they are typically allowed for self-defense purposes. However, the types and calibers of handguns are often restricted, and certain semi-automatic weapons may be prohibited for civilian ownership. **Rifles** are permitted as well, but these are more tightly regulated. To own a rifle, individuals must have a valid reason, such as for hunting or sport. **Shotguns** are another category of legal firearms, mostly used for hunting, though their possession is governed by similar restrictions as rifles.

There are also **limits on the number of firearms** an individual can own. Generally, the law permits ownership of **up to two firearms** per person, though additional weapons may be allowed if the individual can demonstrate a legitimate need, such as for business purposes like operating a

---

10 https://www.puertoplatadr.com/gov/security/personal-defense/

security company. All firearms must be **registered with the government**, ensuring that each weapon can be traced to its lawful owner.

Carrying firearms in public places is more tightly controlled. Even if an individual legally owns a firearm, they are not automatically authorized to carry it in public. **Concealed carry** is possible but requires a **separate permit**, and individuals without the proper permit are prohibited from carrying firearms in public spaces. Violating these rules, including carrying a weapon without a permit or in restricted areas, can result in severe penalties, including fines or imprisonment.

The laws stipulate that firearms should **only be used for lawful purposes**, such as personal defense, hunting, or sport shooting. Any use of firearms in an unlawful manner—such as during the commission of a crime or in an act of aggression—is met with severe penalties. Firearms may not be discharged in public places or in areas where there is a risk of harming others. This includes firing a weapon recklessly or without due care for public safety. Additionally, using a firearm in an unlawful manner can result in significant legal consequences, including imprisonment. In particular, anyone who uses a firearm to threaten or harm others could face criminal charges, including aggravated assault or attempted murder, depending on the severity of the incident.

The use of firearms for **self-defense** is legally recognized, but the circumstances under which it is justified are narrowly defined. Individuals may only use a firearm in self-defense if they face a direct, immediate threat to their life or bodily harm, and the use of force must be proportionate to the threat posed. The use of a firearm in such situations is subject to legal review, and excessive or unjustified use of force can result in criminal charges.

Firearm Restrictions for Visitors

In the Dominican Republic, visitors are **not permitted to bring firearms into the country**. The laws surrounding firearms are strictly enforced, and only Dominican citizens or legal residents can apply for firearm permits. Non-citizens, including tourists, are prohibited from possessing, carrying, or using firearms during their stay.

Those found in violation of these laws face serious legal consequences, including **arrest, fines**, and **possible deportation**. Even if a visitor legally owns a firearm in their home country, they cannot bring it into the Dominican Republic unless they are part of a diplomatic or law enforcement mission, and they must follow the strict procedures outlined by the government for such cases.

 **Penalties**

In the Dominican Republic, firearm-related penalties are taken very seriously, and violations can lead to severe consequences, including imprisonment, fines, and the confiscation of weapons. The penalties vary depending on the nature of the offense.

Possessing a firearm without the necessary permit is a **criminal offense**, and individuals found guilty can face **imprisonment of up to five years** and fines. For those carrying firearms in public without the proper permit, the penalties are similarly harsh, often involving **detention, fines**, and **potential imprisonment** depending on the circumstances.

If someone is caught using a firearm in the commission of a crime, such as assault or robbery, the penalties are even more severe. In these cases, the individual could face **lengthy prison sentences** that can range from **five to 20 years**, depending on the seriousness of the crime and whether the firearm was used in a violent act.

Firearm trafficking is also a serious offense in the Dominican Republic, with penalties designed to deter illegal arms trade. Individuals found guilty of trafficking firearms, either for sale or distribution, face **heavy prison terms** that can last for decades, depending on the quantity and nature of the firearms involved. Additionally, **heavy fines** may be imposed.

The illegal use of firearms, such as firing a weapon in public, can lead to penalties such as **detention, fines**, and **possibly imprisonment** for up to five years. Public safety is a priority, so law enforcement treats any public misuse of a firearm with utmost seriousness.

 **General Questions**

1. *What happens if the police catch me carrying a firearm in the Dominican Republic?* If the police catch you carrying a firearm in the Dominican Republic without a proper license, your weapon will be confiscated, and you could face **imprisonment** for **up to five years** and significant fines. Carrying a firearm in restricted areas, such as near schools, can result in even harsher penalties. It's essential to have a legal permit and follow all regulations to avoid these severe consequences.

2. *Can I bring my gun with me when traveling in the Dominican Republic?* **No.** You generally cannot bring your gun with you when traveling to the Dominican Republic unless you obtain a **special permit** from the Ministry of the Interior and Police, which involves a strict application process. This process requires detailed documentation, including proof of legal ownership, a valid reason for bringing the firearm, and a thorough background check. Even with the proper permits, travelers may face restrictions on carrying the firearm and must comply with strict regulations about storage and transportation. Failure to adhere to these regulations can result in serious legal consequences. It is advisable for travelers to consult with local authorities or their embassy before attempting to bring a firearm into the country.

 **Law of the Land True Story**

Tampa Bay Rays shortstop Wander Franco, already facing charges of sexual abuse involving a 14-year-old girl, was arrested in the Dominican Republic in November 2024 for his involvement in an armed altercation. The altercation occurred over a dispute involving a woman, with police discovering a Glock pistol in Franco's vehicle. The gun, which was registered to his uncle, was found along with 15 rounds of ammunition. Although no injuries were reported, and both parties involved in the altercation agreed not to press charges, the 23-year-old Franco faces charges of illegally carrying a firearm, which could result in a prison sentence of three to five years. The case is ongoing as of the publication of this book.

 **Takeaways**

- Firearm ownership is allowed only for citizens and legal residents who meet specific requirements, including background checks, medical evaluations, and safety courses, with approval from the Ministry of the Interior and Police.

- Tourists and non-citizens cannot bring firearms into the country, and violations can result in arrest, fines, or deportation.

- Violating firearm laws can lead to imprisonment, fines, and weapon confiscation, with harsher penalties for offenses like carrying without a permit or using firearms in crimes.

- Ownership is restricted to handguns, shotguns, and rifles, with regulations on types, calibers, and purposes like self-defense and hunting. Concealed carry requires a separate permit.

- Firearms can be used in self-defense only when facing an immediate threat, and the response must be proportional to the danger.

CHAPTER 7

PROSTITUTION

IN THIS CHAPTER

- Overview
- Laws and Penalties
- Prostitution Practices
- Sex Trafficking and Exploitation
- Sex Tourism and Public Health
- Tips to Avoid Being Solicited
- Law of the Land Hypothetical
- Takeaways

CHAPTER 7

PROSTITUTION

Overview[11]

Prostitution is a complex issue shaped by poverty, economic inequality, gender disparity, and the demand created by sex tourism. While prostitution itself is **not criminalized** in the Dominican Republic, the country has laws targeting human trafficking and sexual exploitation. Many individuals, particularly women, turn to sex work due to limited job opportunities and low wages, with rural-to-urban migration further exacerbating the problem. The country's thriving tourism industry, especially in areas like Punta Cana and Santo Domingo, drives a large demand for sex work, with tourists seeking out cheap and accessible services.

Poverty and **gender inequality** leave many women with few economic choices, while **limited access to education** and skills training makes them vulnerable to exploitation. Efforts to address prostitution focus on public health, such as HIV prevention and outreach programs, though sex workers often remain marginalized and at risk. While there is ongoing debate about decriminalizing or regulating prostitution, the issue remains contentious. Without significant investment in education, economic opportunities, and gender equality, the root causes of prostitution in the Dominican Republic are unlikely to change.

---

11 https://en.wikipedia.org/wiki/Prostitution_in_the_Dominican_Republic

Laws and Penalties

In the Dominican Republic, prostitution itself is **not criminalized**, meaning that engaging in sex work is **not explicitly illegal**. However, the law regulates **related activities**, such as **human trafficking, sexual exploitation**, and **child prostitution**. While there are no designated or officially recognized "zones" for prostitution, certain areas, particularly in tourist-heavy cities like Santo Domingo, Punta Cana, and Puerto Plata, have **informal "red-light" districts** where prostitution is more visible. These areas often operate under a de facto **tolerance by local authorities**, meaning the police may not actively enforce laws against prostitution, but they also don't officially sanction it. These informal zones are often in tourist areas where the demand for sex work is high, and they tend to exist as part of the larger underground economy catering to foreign visitors.

There are **no formal requirements** or official regulations that sex workers must adhere to. However, some public health measures exist, such as **condom distribution** and **HIV/AIDS awareness campaigns**, which are aimed at reducing the spread of sexually transmitted infections (STIs). These efforts are part of broader public health initiatives, but they are not mandatory for sex workers. There are no formal registration or licensing processes for sex workers, and they remain largely outside the scope of the law.

In terms of **penalties for prostitution-related infractions**, penalties are more likely to be applied to activities such as **trafficking** and **exploitation**, rather than to those who engage in sex work voluntarily. Laws around human trafficking are strict, with severe penalties for those involved in exploiting others for sex. Under Dominican law, trafficking, especially involving minors, can result in long prison sentences. Those found guilty of running brothels or exploiting sex workers can face significant legal consequences, including imprisonment. Police may also intervene if prostitution activities are seen as a public nuisance or are in violation of public decency laws, but penalties for individual sex workers are rarely enforced unless they are caught in the act of exploitation or trafficking.

Prostitution Practices

Prostitution in the Dominican Republic is a significant part of the country's informal economy, particularly due to the **widespread influence of sex tourism**. While there are no exact statistics on the total number of sex workers, it is estimated that thousands of people, predominantly women, are involved in prostitution, with the numbers fluctuating in line with the seasons, particularly during peak tourist times. The absence of comprehensive data makes it difficult to accurately assess the scale of prostitution in the country, but it is widely acknowledged as a prevalent social issue.

Prostitution in the Dominican Republic exists in various forms, each varying in visibility, organization, and clientele:

- **Street Prostitution:** This is the most visible form of prostitution, where women (and some men) solicit clients on the streets, particularly in urban areas like **Santo Domingo, Puerto Plata**, and **Punta Cana**. Street prostitution is common in tourist districts, often close to bars, nightclubs, and resorts. Women working in this sector are often vulnerable, with limited bargaining power and few protections from exploitation or abuse.

- **Brothels:** Brothels, often operating under the guise of **massage parlors**, **nightclubs**, or **strip clubs**, are another prominent form of prostitution in the Dominican Republic. These establishments are typically located in tourist areas and are often linked to organized crime or unofficial networks. Brothel workers may have more structure and organization compared to street-based sex work, but they often face significant exploitation, with profits largely going to the owners of the brothels or pimps. The police rarely intervene unless there are clear cases of trafficking or forced prostitution.

- **Escort Services:** Escort services are also common, particularly for wealthier tourists or businesspeople visiting the country. These services can be found through **personal connections, hotel concierges**, or **online platforms**. Escorts typically advertise via word of mouth or through specialized websites that connect clients with sex workers. This form of prostitution is less visible than street or brothel work and often involves a higher degree of discretion.

- **Online Prostitution:** The rise of online platforms and social media has introduced new avenues for prostitution in the Dominican Republic. **Websites, dating apps,** and platforms like **Instagram** or **Facebook** have enabled sex workers to advertise their services more discreetly, often catering to a global clientele. Some sex workers in the Dominican Republic may choose to operate independently online, avoiding physical brothels or street work. Online prostitution also allows for a more personalized form of sex work, with the potential for higher earnings through one-on-one encounters or virtual services.

The attitude of local authorities toward prostitution is **ambivalent**, shaped by a mix of social, cultural, and economic factors. On one hand, prostitution is **largely tolerated** in specific areas, particularly those catering to tourists. In popular tourist destinations like Punta Cana and Santo Domingo, prostitution is often seen as a **necessary part of the local economy**, contributing to the informal sector that supports the tourism industry. Local authorities generally turn a blind eye to sex work in these zones, allowing the trade to flourish as long as it doesn't disturb public order.

However, prostitution is still viewed as **socially taboo** in many parts of Dominican society. Conservative views on sexuality, influenced by Catholicism and traditional values, lead to a **moral stigma** surrounding sex work. As a result, sex workers often face discrimination, exclusion, and marginalization from broader society. The authorities focus their efforts on **combating trafficking**, especially of minors, and addressing exploitation in brothels and other illicit establishments. They may also crack down on activities that **disrupt public order**, such as street solicitation in non-designated areas or near schools. Local police may sometimes **raid brothels** or **escort agencies** suspected of exploiting sex workers, particularly when trafficking or other illegal activities are suspected. However, for the most part, authorities choose to focus on organized crime and trafficking networks rather than the sex workers themselves.

Sex Trafficking and Exploitation[12]

Sex trafficking and exploitation are **major concerns** in the Dominican Republic, driven by a combination of poverty, gender inequality, and the country's role as a top sex tourism destination. The demand for prostitution in tourist areas like **Punta Cana**, **Santo Domingo**, and **Puerto Plata** fuels trafficking networks that exploit **women** and **children**. Many trafficked individuals are lured with false promises of work or a better life, only to be forced into prostitution, often in tourist-heavy regions. The country's vulnerability is heightened by its role as a destination for sex tourists and a source of migrants, who are at risk of exploitation.

The most vulnerable populations include **young women**, **children**, and **migrants**. These individuals, particularly from impoverished or rural areas, are often targeted by traffickers offering fake employment opportunities. Migrants, especially from Haiti, are particularly at risk due to their precarious legal and economic status.

The Dominican government has enacted **anti-trafficking laws** and partnered with international organizations like **Interpol** and the **UN** to combat trafficking. Efforts also include **public awareness campaigns** and **support services for victims**. However, enforcement remains **inconsistent**, and traffickers continue to exploit vulnerable individuals, particularly in tourist areas. While some victim support systems exist, gaps remain in **reintegration programs**, leaving survivors vulnerable to re-trafficking.

 ## Sex Tourism and Public Health

Sex tourism is quite **widespread** in the Dominican Republic, with the country being **one of the top destinations** for sex tourists in the

---

12   https://en.wikipedia.org/wiki/
Human_trafficking_in_the_Dominican_Republic

Caribbean and Latin America. The influx of foreign visitors, especially from countries like the United States, Canada, and European nations, has made the Dominican Republic a hub for sex tourism. This phenomenon is not only driven by the affordability of services but also by the country's large informal economy, where prostitution is often tolerated or overlooked by local authorities.

The most prominent destinations for sex tourism in the Dominican Republic are **Punta Cana, Santo Domingo, Puerto Plata**, and **Bávaro**. These areas attract large numbers of international tourists, particularly those seeking **cheap and accessible sexual services**. Punta Cana and Bávaro, in particular, are well-known for their all-inclusive resorts, where tourists may engage in sex tourism activities within a more discrete or controlled environment. **Santo Domingo**, as the capital, is also a hotspot, with numerous bars, clubs, and informal areas where sex work is visible and often directly linked to tourism. Likewise, **Puerto Plata** and other coastal towns cater to similar demands, with sex work present in the form of street prostitution, brothels, and escort services.

Sex tourism in the Dominican Republic is often **informally organized**, typically operating within the broader tourism infrastructure. Many tourists seeking sex work do so through local **brokers, bars, nightclubs**, and **massage parlors** that serve as fronts for prostitution. **Escort services** are another common way that sex tourism is arranged, where tourists contact sex workers directly, often through word-of-mouth, or through hotel concierges who may discreetly help to facilitate arrangements.

Online platforms have also emerged as a significant tool for advertising and organizing sex tourism. **Websites, social media pages**, and apps like **Tinder** or **Instagram** have allowed sex workers in the Dominican Republic to directly reach potential clients, bypassing traditional in-person solicitation.

Local **brothel owners** or **pimps** often play a role in organizing and advertising sex tourism, providing a supply of women and escort services to meet the demand from tourists. These services are often not advertised publicly but are known in local circles, and they tend to be linked to areas where prostitution is tolerated. Word-of-mouth, local knowledge, and online platforms are the primary ways in which sex tourists find these services.

As elsewhere, sex tourism in the Dominican Republic raises several significant public health and safety concerns. These include the spread of sexually transmitted infections (STIs), including HIV, due to unprotected sex and limited healthcare access for those involved. Human trafficking, particularly for sexual exploitation, is a major issue, with both minors and adults at risk of abuse and coercion. The industry is also linked to organized crime, increasing the risk of violence and exploitation for sex workers. Socially, sex tourism exacerbates economic inequality, creates a cycle of poverty, and normalizes exploitation, while negatively impacting local communities and family structures. Legal gaps and corruption within law enforcement make it difficult to address these issues effectively. Additionally, the mental and physical health of sex workers often suffers due to stigma, abuse, and lack of support.

 ## Tips to Avoid Being Solicited

When traveling to the Dominican Republic, it's important to be mindful of your surroundings and take steps to avoid unwanted attention or solicitation. While the country is known for its beautiful beaches and vibrant culture, some areas may attract individuals looking to engage tourists in various forms of solicitation. Here are some practical tips to help you avoid being solicited during your trip:

- Choose reputable hotels and resorts in safe, tourist-friendly neighborhoods to minimize encounters with sex workers.

- If approached, politely but firmly say no and walk away. Avoid engaging in conversation.

- Stay clear of areas known for high levels of solicitation, especially at night, such as certain bars or secluded parts of beaches.

- Overindulging in alcohol can make you more vulnerable to unwanted attention. Stay aware of your surroundings.

- Avoid drawing attention by dressing too flashy or expensive. Keep valuables hidden.

- Stick to official taxis or ride-sharing apps, especially after dark, to avoid being targeted in less secure areas.

 ## Law of the Land Hypothetical

HYPOTHETICAL: *John, a tourist visiting the Dominican Republic, is staying at a popular all-inclusive resort in Punta Cana. While enjoying his time at the resort's beach, he is approached by a woman offering her services. John politely declines and walks away, but the woman continues to follow him, making repeated offers. Feeling uncomfortable, John decides to report the incident to the hotel staff and ask for advice on how to handle the situation if it happens again. Does John have legal recourse for harassment, and what can he do to ensure his safety?*

ANSWER: *While prostitution is not illegal in the Dominican Republic, persistent solicitation can be seen as harassment or a public nuisance. John has the right to refuse and report the behavior to hotel security or local authorities. If the harassment continues, it could violate public decency laws. To avoid further issues, John should stay in secure areas, avoid secluded spots, and use official transportation. Hotel staff can assist in contacting authorities if needed.*

 ## Takeaways

- In the Dominican Republic, prostitution itself is not illegal, but activities like human trafficking, sexual exploitation, and child prostitution are heavily penalized.

- The country's thriving sex tourism industry, particularly in areas like Punta Cana and Santo Domingo, creates significant demand for sex work, often tied to poverty and gender inequality.

- While prostitution is tolerated in certain tourist areas, sex workers often harass tourists, which can lead to uncomfortable situations. Tourists should be firm and report persistent solicitation to authorities or hotel staff.

- The Dominican Republic faces a major issue with sex trafficking, particularly involving vulnerable groups like women, children, and migrants. The government has laws to combat trafficking but enforcement remains inconsistent.

- Sex tourism contributes to the spread of sexually transmitted infections (STIs), including HIV, and creates serious public health risks due to unprotected sex and limited healthcare access for sex workers.

LGBTQ

- Homophobia in the Dominican Republic
- LGBTQ Legislation
- LGBTQ Tourism and Safety Concerns
- General Questions
- Law of the Land True Story
- Law of the Land Hypothetical

LGBTQ

Homophobia in the Dominican Republic[13]

The Dominican Republic has a complex and **historically conservative relationship** with its LGBTQ+ community, influenced by deep-rooted religious beliefs, cultural norms, and political history. During the dictatorship of Rafael Trujillo (1930-1961), LGBTQ+ individuals faced severe repression. Homosexuality was criminalized, and the regime associated it with moral decay. While laws against sodomy were **decriminalized in 1997**, the stigma surrounding LGBTQ+ people persisted for many years. The nation's Catholic foundation, along with the strong influence of evangelical Protestantism, shaped societal views that often condemned same-sex relationships as immoral.

In recent years, while the cultural landscape has slowly shifted, the general attitude toward LGBTQ+ individuals remains conservative, especially outside of urban areas. In places like Santo Domingo, **more progressive views** have taken root, particularly among younger generations, yet many Dominicans still view LGBTQ+ issues with discomfort or outright hostility. Many LGBTQ+ individuals remain in the shadows to avoid societal exclusion and family rejection, particularly in rural communities where such identities are rarely acknowledged.

---

13 https://humanrightsfirst.org/wp-content/uploads/2022/11/dominican-republic-fact-sheet.pdf

The cultural, social, and religious factors influencing these attitudes are significant. **The Roman Catholic Church** remains an influential institution in Dominican society, often leading opposition to LGBTQ+ rights, and reinforcing the idea that homosexuality is sinful. Evangelical Protestantism has also contributed to negative attitudes, with many religious leaders openly **denouncing LGBTQ+ rights**. Furthermore, the pervasive **"machismo" culture**—characterized by rigid gender expectations—continues to stigmatize anything perceived as deviating from heterosexual norms. This creates a hostile environment for those who identify outside of these conventional roles, contributing to the marginalization and mistreatment of LGBTQ+ individuals.

In daily life, homophobia manifests in various ways. In workplaces, LGBTQ+ individuals may fear **discrimination** or even losing their jobs if their sexual orientation or gender identity is known. In schools, **homophobic bullying** is prevalent, and LGBTQ+ students often face isolation or physical violence. **Family rejection** is another pervasive issue, with many LGBTQ+ individuals enduring emotional or physical abuse after coming out. The lack of open discussions and educational efforts about LGBTQ+ rights means these issues persist largely unchecked.

Reports of violence and discrimination against LGBTQ+ people in the Dominican Republic are common but **underreported**, as fear of further victimization deters many from speaking out. The country has witnessed numerous **attacks on LGBTQ+ individuals**, particularly transgender women, who are often subjected to violence, including murder. A 2020 report by Amnesty International highlighted how the lack of proper data on hate crimes stems from the societal stigma surrounding LGBTQ+ issues. **Police discrimination** is also a problem, with law enforcement often targeting LGBTQ+ people, especially transgender individuals, for arbitrary arrests or abuse.

While homophobic sentiments remain widespread, there are a few **notable public figures** advocating for LGBTQ+ rights. **Amara La Negra**, a singer and reality TV star, has used her platform to support LGBTQ+ rights, focusing on racial and gender equality. **Carlos de la Mota**, an actor, has also spoken out in favor of LGBTQ+ causes. However, these voices are still rare in a society where many public figures, particularly politicians and religious leaders, either oppose LGBTQ+ rights or remain silent on the issue, fearing backlash from more conservative sectors of society.

Despite these challenges, there have been signs of progress in recent years. The legal rights of LGBTQ+ individuals have evolved slowly, with some legal protections against discrimination in areas like employment and healthcare being introduced in 2021. However, **same-sex marriage remains illegal**, and the fight for full legal recognition and equal rights continues. The country saw its **first Pride march in 2018**, signaling a growing movement for visibility and acceptance. While Pride events remain controversial in some parts of the country, they are becoming more prominent in urban areas, with larger turnouts each year. International pressure, particularly from human rights organizations, has also spurred some reform, encouraging a shift in policies toward greater inclusivity.

LGBTQ Legislation

Consensual same-sex sexual acts have been legal in the Dominican Republic since 1822. However, Article 210 of the 1966 Police Justice Code and article 260 of the Code of Justice of the Armed Forces still **outlaw "sodomy"** (defined as a "sexual act between persons of the same sex") among members of police forces and military officers, respectively.[14] These articles impose prison sentences of up to two years for police officers and one year for armed forces officers.

Regarding LGBTQ+ rights, the country lacks comprehensive legal protections. **Same-sex marriage** is **not recognized**, as the Dominican Constitution defines marriage as a union between a man and a woman.[15] Additionally, same-sex couples **cannot jointly adopt children**, and there is **no legal recognition of gender identity** for transgender individuals. While there are no laws criminalizing LGBTQ+ people, the country does not offer specific protections in areas like family law, adoption, or

---

14   https://www.hrw.org/news/2024/08/30/
     dominican-republic-court-reviews-laws-against-gay-sex

15   https://humanrightsfirst.org/wp-content/uploads/2022/11/domini-
     can-republic-fact-sheet.pdf

gender identity, leaving the LGBTQ+ community vulnerable to legal and social challenges.

There are few legal instruments that protect LGBTQ people from discrimination in the Dominican Republic. The **General Law on Youth** (Law 49/2000) prohibits discrimination based on sexual orientation since 2000. **Article 11** of the Code of Criminal Procedure, effective since 2007, requires judges and prosecutors to consider the circumstances of each person but not base decisions solely on sexual orientation. **Law 135/2011** on HIV/AIDS has prohibited discrimination based on sexual orientation and gender identity since 2011. And although the Constitution guarantees equal rights, it does not specifically mention sexual orientation or gender identity. As a result, LGBTQ+ individuals lack legal protection from discrimination in areas such as employment, housing, healthcare, government services and education. However, there are no explicit laws that ban discrimination based on sexual orientation.

Hate crimes motivated by sexual orientation or gender identity are also **not explicitly recognized**, though violent acts could potentially be prosecuted under general anti-violence laws.[16]

The level of support for LGBTQ+ rights varies significantly depending on the region. In **urban areas** like Santo Domingo and Santiago, the LGBTQ+ community is more visible and active, and there are spaces that are more accepting, including LGBTQ+-friendly businesses and organizations. Events such as the annual **Santo Domingo Pride Parade**, though controversial, reflect a degree of progress in the capital. Additionally, activist organizations such as **Diversidad Dominicana, Amigos Siempre Amigos**, and **Trans Siempre Amigas** are working to promote LGBTQ+ rights and provide support.[17] However, **rural areas** tend to be **less supportive**, with more conservative attitudes that can lead to significant social and legal challenges for LGBTQ+ individuals.

---

16   https://en.wikipedia.org/wiki/
LGBTQ_rights_in_the_Dominican_Republic

17   https://pisqueya.com/blogs/news/it-s-not-all-sunshine-beach-
es-for-lgbtq-in-the-dominican-republic?srsltid=AfmBOopINqIaJHn-
qLioQlSGrZ7e_06nGjvTrhEK6TgUFA2IbLe7I8Q7e

Religious influence in the country, particularly from the Roman Catholic Church and evangelical groups, further contributes to the opposition to LGBTQ+ rights, reinforcing conservative societal views.

LGBTQ Tourism and Safety Concerns[18]

LGBTQ+ tourism in the Dominican Republic is still in its **early stages**. While the country is not as advanced in terms of LGBTQ+ tourism as other destinations in the Caribbean, there is a growing interest in attracting LGBTQ+ visitors, particularly in urban areas and tourist-centric regions like Santo Domingo, Punta Cana, and Cabarete. In these areas, there is a limited but **growing number of LGBTQ+-friendly establishments** such as bars, clubs, and resorts that cater to LGBTQ+ tourists. However, the country does not yet host large-scale LGBTQ+ events or pride parades, though smaller gatherings and community events are becoming more common in major cities.

Tolerance toward the LGBTQ+ community in the Dominican Republic **varies significantly**, depending on the region. Urban areas, especially Santo Domingo and Santiago, are generally more accepting and open to LGBTQ+ individuals compared to smaller towns or rural areas, where conservative and religious views are more prevalent. In the larger cities, there is a more visible LGBTQ+ presence, and some businesses and venues are welcoming to LGBTQ+ visitors. However, in rural or smaller towns, where traditional values hold greater sway, LGBTQ+ individuals may face social ostracism or hostility, and visitors in these areas should be cautious about expressing their sexuality or gender identity.[19]

Public displays of affection between LGBTQ+ individuals are generally **not widely accepted** throughout the country. In major cities, there may be some tolerance for less overt forms of affection, such as holding hands, but any public displays of affection that are more obvious may attract unwanted attention or negative reactions, especially in less touristy

---

18 https://canatransfers.com/punta-cana/lgbtq-travel-in-punta-cana/

19 https://aperian.com/blog/
local-diversity-and-inclusion-spotlight-the-dominican-republic

areas. Visitors in major tourist resorts or LGBTQ+-friendly venues may have more freedom to express themselves, but it's always advisable to be discreet when outside of these safe spaces, particularly in more conservative areas.

Safety concerns for LGBTQ+ visitors do exist, especially if they are not cautious about their behavior or where they go. While instances of violence specifically targeting LGBTQ+ tourists are rare, **discrimination and harassment remain significant risks.** LGBTQ+ individuals may experience **verbal harassment, unwanted attention,** or even **physical intimidation,** especially in areas where the community is less visible or accepted. Though the Dominican Republic does not have laws actively targeting LGBTQ+ people, the lack of legal protections and widespread societal acceptance means that LGBTQ+ visitors should be mindful of their surroundings. Sexual harassment can also be a concern, particularly for LGBTQ+ men in tourist-heavy areas, where some individuals may attempt to exploit them. As with any destination, being aware of local customs and cultural sensitivities is essential. The Dominican Republic is a predominantly conservative society, and LGBTQ+ visitors are encouraged to approach their interactions with respect for local norms. Staying in LGBTQ+-friendly accommodations, avoiding overly public displays of affection, and being cautious in less tolerant areas are key for ensuring a safer and more enjoyable visit.

 **General Questions**

1. *Do laws in the Dominican Republic protect homosexual expressions and conduct?* **No.** Laws in the Dominican Republic do not specifically protect homosexual expressions and conduct. While consensual same-sex relationships between adults are not criminalized, there are no comprehensive legal protections for LGBTQ+ individuals. There are no anti-discrimination laws covering sexual orientation or gender identity, meaning LGBTQ+ people may face discrimination in areas like employment, housing, and healthcare. Same-sex marriage is not recognized, and transgender individuals struggle with legal recognition.

2. *What is the penalty for homosexual expressions and conduct?* **There is no legal penalty** for homosexual expressions and conduct in the Dominican Republic. Consensual same-sex activity between adults is not criminalized, and there are no specific laws that penalize homosexual behavior. However, while same-sex conduct is not punishable by law, LGBTQ+ individuals may face social stigma, discrimination, or harassment, particularly in more conservative areas.

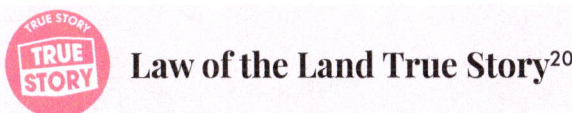 **Law of the Land True Story[20]**

In October 2014, Van Teasley, a prominent gay D.C. defense attorney, was found murdered in his vacation apartment in Santo Domingo, Dominican Republic. The 55-year-old was discovered bound, gagged, and strangled, with no signs of forced entry. Police launched a homicide investigation, though the motive remained unclear. Some speculated

---

20 https://www.washingtonblade.com/2014/11/04/
    gay-d-c-attorney-slain-dominican-republic/

that the murder might have been motivated by his sexual orientation, with the possibility that Teasley was targeted because he was gay.

Teasley was well-known for his work representing low-income gay and transgender clients and was a respected figure in the LGBT community. He had worked with organizations like Transgender Health Empowerment and HIPS, mentoring LGBT individuals, including those in recovery. An advocate for LGBT rights, Teasley had testified in 2008 about the need to address hate crimes against the community. His death shocked both his legal peers and the community he served.

 **Law of the Land Hypothetical**

HYPOTHETICAL: *Mariana, a 32-year-old transgender woman, travels to Punta Cana for a vacation. While visiting a local resort, she faces discrimination from hotel staff, who refuse to address her by her preferred name and pronouns, despite her clear communication. Mariana feels humiliated.*

Can Mariana seek legal recourse for discrimination based on gender identity in the Dominican Republic?

ANSWER: *In the Dominican Republic, there are no specific legal protections for gender identity under anti-discrimination laws. While some laws prohibit discrimination based on sexual orientation, gender identity is not explicitly mentioned. Mariana can file a complaint with the resort management or the Ministry of Tourism, particularly if the resort is part of an international chain with anti-discrimination policies. Legal action is uncertain due to the lack of clear protections, but she can also reach out to advocacy groups like Trans Siempre Amigas to seek support or public attention for her case. While the legal system may offer limited recourse, public or organizational pressure could be a key strategy.*

SEXUALLY MOTIVATED/ VIOLENT CRIMES

IN THIS CHAPTER

- Overview
- Related Legislation
- General Questions
- Law of the Land Hypothetical
- Takeaways

CHAPTER 9

SEXUALLY MOTIVATED/ VIOLENT CRIMES

Overview

Sexually motivated crimes, including sexual assault, harassment, and violence, are prevalent in the Dominican Republic, though comprehensive statistics are difficult to obtain due to underreporting and insufficient data collection. Sexual violence, particularly against women and LGBTQ+ individuals, remains a **significant issue**. Transgender people, especially transgender women, are at heightened risk of violence and sexual abuse. While reliable statistics are scarce, organizations like the United Nations and Amnesty International have highlighted the ongoing problem of sexual violence in the country. Reports from UN Women suggest that one in three women in the Dominican Republic experiences sexual violence in their lifetime, although such incidents are often underreported, especially in rural areas.

The prevalence of sexually motivated crimes can be attributed to several social, cultural, and economic factors. The **"machismo" culture**, which promotes male dominance and rigid gender roles, often normalizes sexual aggression and violence, particularly when the victim is a woman or a member of the LGBTQ+ community. The influence of the **Roman Catholic Church** and **evangelical Protestantism** contributes to conservative views on gender and sexuality, reinforcing patriarchal norms that may downplay the severity of sexual violence. **Economic disparity** also plays a role; poverty, especially among women, LGBTQ+ individuals, and rural populations, makes people more vulnerable to sexual exploitation and abuse. The lack of resources, education, and support systems further exacerbates the vulnerability of these groups. Additionally, there is a significant barrier to reporting crimes due to fear of social stigma, retaliation, or police indifference. Transgender individuals, in particular, may avoid reporting due to concerns about **police discrimination or abuse**.

Women are the most affected by sexually motivated crimes in the Dominican Republic. They face high rates of sexual violence, harassment, and exploitation, with domestic violence, including sexual violence within relationships, being particularly common. **LGBTQ+ individuals**, especially transgender women, are also disproportionately targeted by sexual violence. They face higher rates of physical and sexual assault, driven by a lack of legal protections and societal acceptance. **Rural populations** are at an even greater disadvantage, as they often have limited access to resources, weaker law enforcement, and more conservative attitudes that normalize sexual violence. Although **tourists** face a lower risk, there have been incidents of sexual violence against foreign visitors, particularly in tourist areas where exploitation and abuse can go unreported.

Regional differences are significant when considering the prevalence of sexually motivated crimes. In urban areas like Santo Domingo and Santiago, sexual violence is more likely to be reported due to a larger population and greater awareness of the issue. Civil society organizations in these cities are pushing for better data collection and stronger justice mechanisms for victims. In contrast, rural regions experience higher rates of underreporting, and conservative cultural and religious attitudes in these areas may contribute to the normalization of sexual violence. Rural areas also tend to have fewer resources for victims and weaker law enforcement. Tourist-heavy regions such as Punta Cana and Cabarete present unique challenges, as the presence of resorts and bars can create environments where sexual exploitation and harassment are more likely to occur. In these areas, local authorities may prioritize economic interests, making it harder to address crimes targeting vulnerable populations, including tourists and LGBTQ+ individuals.

Related Legislation

In the Dominican Republic, there are laws that criminalize various forms of sexual violence, including rape, harassment, and trafficking. **Rape** is punishable by **10 to 20 years in prison**, and the Domestic Violence Law (Law 24-97) addresses violence within family settings, including sexual violence, providing protective measures and penalties. However, the **enforcement** of these laws is **often weak** due to underreporting, societal stigma, and a lack of resources within the judicial system.

Domestic violence, including sexual violence within intimate relationships, remains prevalent, and cultural attitudes, particularly the "machismo" culture, often result in victim-blaming and hinder accountability for perpetrators. **Sexual harassment** is prohibited but not comprehensively addressed by national laws, especially in the workplace or public spaces. The penalties for harassment are vague and enforcement is inconsistent, especially when powerful individuals are involved.

Despite the existence of relevant laws, enforcement remains weak due to systemic issues such as corruption, inefficiency, and a lack of proper police training. Victims, especially in rural or conservative areas, may face social stigma, retaliation, or a lack of legal support, making them less likely to report crimes. In tourist areas, local authorities sometimes prioritize the region's reputation over addressing cases of sexual violence, leading to underreporting or dismissal of cases.

General Questions

1. ***Do laws in the Dominican Republic related to sex crimes protect the victims equally?*** **No.** Laws related to sex crimes in the Dominican Republic are designed to protect victims, but their application is inconsistent, and there are significant gaps in their effectiveness. While the criminal code defines sexual violence and harassment and provides for penalties, enforcement is often weak. Victims may face challenges such as insufficient support services, delays in the judicial system, and a lack of specialized training for law enforcement. Cultural factors, such as victim-blaming and gender biases, also hinder equal protection. Consequently, while the laws theoretically provide protection, many victims, especially women and marginalized groups, do not experience equal treatment in practice.

2. ***Pursuant to law, what is the age of consent for sex in the Dominican Republic?*** In the Dominican Republic, the legal age of consent for sexual activity is **18 years old**. However, the law allows for some exceptions, such as when both individuals are close in age. If one party is between the ages of 16 and 18 and the other is no more than five years older, the sexual relationship is considered legal. Despite these legal provisions, there are concerns about the enforcement of age of consent laws, particularly in rural areas where underage pregnancies and sexual exploitation still occur.

Law of the Land Hypothetical

HYPOTHETICAL: *Lucía, a 19-year-old Dominican citizen, is harassed at a nightclub in Santo Domingo by a man who makes inappropriate sexual advances. Despite her refusal, he continues, touching her and making lewd comments. Lucía manages to push him away and escapes. Feeling shaken, she decides to report the incident. She has witness statements from her friends and a photo of the man. What should Lucía do to ensure the harassment is properly addressed under Dominican law, and what legal protections are available to her?*

ANSWER: *Lucía should report the incident to the nearest police station in Santo Domingo, providing all evidence, including the photo and witness statements. Sexual harassment is punishable under Dominican law, and the police must investigate. She should file a formal complaint and request follow-up action. Consulting a lawyer can help her navigate the legal process and ensure her rights are upheld. Additionally, Lucía may seek emotional support through counseling. By taking these steps, she can ensure the case is taken seriously and legal action is pursued.*

 **Takeaways**

- Sexual violence, particularly against women and LGBTQ+ individuals, is widespread in the Dominican Republic. One in three women experiences sexual violence in their lifetime, with underreporting being a significant issue.

- The "machismo" culture and rigid gender roles normalize sexual violence, especially in rural areas. Economic disparity, particularly among women and LGBTQ+ individuals, increases vulnerability to exploitation and abuse.

- Women face high rates of sexual violence, harassment, and exploitation. LGBTQ+ individuals, especially transgender women, are disproportionately targeted. Rural populations have even less access to resources and weaker law enforcement, making them more vulnerable.

- Urban areas like Santo Domingo and Santiago have better reporting mechanisms and support systems for victims. Rural areas and tourist regions face higher rates of underreporting, and local authorities may prioritize economic interests over addressing crimes.

- While there are laws criminalizing sexual violence, including rape and harassment, enforcement is weak due to systemic issues like corruption and inefficiency. Cultural factors such as victim-blaming also hinder effective protection and justice for victims.

CHAPTER 10

ARRESTED IN THE DOMINICAN REPUBLIC

IN THIS CHAPTER

- Overview
- Arrest Process
- Rights of the Arrested Person
- Getting Legal Assistance
- Bail
- Complaints Against Police
- General Questions
- Law of the Land True Story

ARRESTED IN THE DOMINICAN REPUBLIC

Overview

When traveling in a foreign country, it's imperative to recognize that you are subject to the legal jurisdiction and regulations of that nation. These laws may significantly differ from those in your home country and might not offer the same legal protections you are accustomed to. It's crucial to bear in mind that penalties for violating foreign laws can be more severe than those for similar offenses in your home country, and ignorance of these laws is not typically accepted as a defense.

The consequences for breaking the law while abroad can be severe and may include expulsion, fines, arrest, or imprisonment. Even unintentional violations can lead to serious legal repercussions. It is essential for travelers to be aware of and adhere to the laws of the host country to avoid legal entanglements and ensure a safe and enjoyable experience.

Specifically, stringent penalties are often enforced for possession, use, or trafficking of illegal drugs in many countries. Convicted offenders can expect severe consequences, including lengthy jail sentences and hefty fines. The legal processes for foreigners in the event of an arrest abroad involve being charged or indicted, prosecuted, potentially convicted and sentenced, and, if applicable, going through an appeals process.

Navigating a foreign legal system can be complex, and individuals arrested abroad must be prepared to comply with the legal procedures of the host country. Seeking legal representation and understanding the local legal nuances are crucial steps for those facing legal issues in a foreign jurisdiction.

Awareness of and adherence to the laws of a foreign country are paramount when traveling. Understanding the potential consequences for legal violations and being prepared to navigate the legal system of the host country are essential aspects of responsible international travel.

Arrest Process[21]

The arrest process in the Dominican Republic follows a structured legal procedure, and understanding the process is crucial for both locals and foreigners. The legal system allows for arrests based on a wide range of criminal charges, including drug-related offenses, theft, assault, fraud, sexual offenses, traffic violations, and even homicide. Each charge carries its own level of severity and potential consequences.

Arrests in the Dominican Republic can occur **with** or **without a warrant**. If a crime is witnessed by the police or if there is sufficient evidence that a crime has been committed, officers can arrest someone immediately without the need for a warrant. Alternatively, if there is enough suspicion or probable cause, a judge can issue an arrest warrant based on evidence provided by the police. Once the individual is **detained**, they are brought to a police station where their personal details are recorded, and they may undergo an initial questioning. At this stage, the individual has the right to remain silent and to request legal representation. If they cannot afford a lawyer, a public defender will be assigned to them.

The next stage in the process is the **Rule of 48**, which mandates that an individual must appear before a judge **within 48 hours** of being arrested. This is to ensure that individuals are not held in custody for longer

---

21   https://travel.gc.ca/travelling/advisories/dominican-republic/
     criminal-law-system

than necessary without formal legal oversight. The judge will review the evidence, and based on this, they will decide whether to continue holding the person in custody or release them, either with or without bail. If the person is not released, they may remain in pretrial detention as the investigation continues.

Following the judge's review, the prosecutor leads **the investigation**. The prosecutor is responsible for gathering evidence, questioning witnesses, and determining whether formal charges should be pressed. If there is enough evidence, the case will proceed to **trial**. If not, the charges can be dropped. During the trial, a judge or panel of judges will evaluate the evidence and testimonies. If the accused is found guilty, a sentence will be handed down, which could range from a fine to imprisonment, depending on the crime.

Rights of the Arrested Person[22]

In the Dominican Republic, the rights of an arrested person are safeguarded by the Constitution, the Criminal Procedure Code, and international human rights agreements. Upon arrest, an individual has the **right to be informed of the charges** against them. This means they must be told the reasons for their arrest and any evidence being used to justify it in a language they understand.

The arrested person also has the right to **legal representation**. They may appoint their own lawyer or, if unable to afford one, the state will provide a public defender. Furthermore, the arrested individual has the **right to remain silent** during any questioning, meaning they cannot be forced to incriminate themselves. Any statements made under coercion are inadmissible in court.

Additionally, the arrested person **must be brought before a judge within 48 hours**. If no formal charges are filed within that time frame, they must be released. The arrested person is also guaranteed **humane**

---

22 https://travel.gc.ca/travelling/advisories/dominican-republic/
    criminal-law-system

treatment, meaning they cannot be subjected to torture or degrading conditions.

The individual has the **right to communicate** with their family or a third party, such as a legal representative, to inform them of their arrest. This is especially important for foreigners, who also have the right to request **consular assistance** from their home country's embassy or consulate. If necessary, an interpreter should be provided if the arrested person does not speak Spanish, ensuring they can understand the legal process and communicate effectively.

Medical assistance is another important right. If the arrested individual is injured or ill, they are entitled to receive medical attention, whether in detention or at a healthcare facility.

For **foreigners** arrested in the Dominican Republic, there are some **specific considerations.** Foreign nationals are entitled to **consular assistance**, meaning they can contact their embassy for help. The embassy ensures that the individual is treated fairly under Dominican law and may provide guidance on legal procedures. However, the language barrier can be a significant issue, as Spanish is the official language. Non-Spanish speakers may struggle to understand the proceedings, which makes having **a translator** or legal representative who speaks both Spanish and the foreigner's language crucial.

Legal representation is another important aspect. Foreign nationals can hire a **private lawyer** or, if they cannot afford one, a **public defender** will be assigned. However, due to the complexity of the Dominican legal system and the potential for misunderstandings, especially when a foreigner is involved, it's often advisable to hire a lawyer familiar with the local laws and customs. In cases involving serious charges, having a local attorney can help ensure the individual's rights are protected.

Getting Legal Assistance[23]

The **Constitution of the Dominican Republic** guarantees every arrested person the right to legal assistance. This means that upon arrest, the individual has the right to have a lawyer represent them throughout the criminal process. If the person cannot afford a lawyer, they are entitled to a public defender provided by the state. This right ensures that no one, regardless of their financial situation, is left without legal support. In addition to the right to a lawyer, arrested persons are also informed of their right to remain silent during questioning, preventing any self-incrimination. The **Criminal Procedure Code** further ensures that this right is protected at all stages of the legal process, from arrest through to trial.

If you are arrested in the Dominican Republic, it is important to assert your rights from the outset. First, ask to speak with a lawyer. You have the right to legal representation, and if you cannot afford one, the government will provide a **public defender**. Additionally, it is crucial to assert your **right to remain silent** and avoid answering questions that could incriminate you before you have consulted with your lawyer. If you do not speak Spanish, ask for an interpreter immediately, as this will help ensure that you understand the charges and the legal process.

You should also inform the authorities that you are a foreign national and request that your **embassy or consulate** be notified of your arrest. This is your right under international law, and your embassy can assist you in navigating the legal system, ensuring that your treatment complies with international standards. If the authorities do not automatically notify your embassy, you have the right to do so yourself. Lastly, if you are injured or feel unwell, you should request medical assistance, as you are entitled to receive medical care during detention if necessary.

Your **embassy or consulate** plays a crucial role in protecting your rights during the arrest process in the Dominican Republic. Although consular representatives cannot interfere directly with the legal process, they

---

23 https://wdalaw.com/criminal-law/what-to-do-if-you-are-arrested-or-detained-in-dominican-republic.php

can provide vital assistance to ensure that you are treated fairly and that your legal rights are respected. They will help you understand the local legal system, assist you in finding a qualified lawyer, and provide you with information on your rights during detention. The consulate will also monitor your detention to ensure that you are not subjected to **inhumane treatment** or **unfair legal procedures**. If necessary, the consular staff can facilitate communication with your family or loved ones and offer support in case of diplomatic intervention, particularly in more serious cases where there may be concerns about the fairness of the trial or your treatment.

It is important to understand that the embassy or consulate cannot directly influence the outcome of the legal process or secure your release, but they can ensure that you are being treated according to the law and can offer valuable guidance throughout the process.

Beyond your home embassy, you can get legal assistance in the Dominican Republic by contacting the **Colegio de Abogados de la República Dominicana** (https://card.org.do/) for lawyer referrals, visiting **university legal clinics** like those at PUCMM or UNIBE for free or low-cost help, or working with a **Notario Público**, who is a licensed attorney for paperwork and contracts but not court cases. Online platforms like **LexLatin** also list lawyers offering virtual consultations, and NGOs such as **Centro Bono** provide free or low-cost legal aid, especially in human rights and immigration cases.

Bail[24]

While the Dominican Republic does have a bail system, it operates with certain restrictions, particularly for serious crimes. The country's **Criminal Procedure Code** outlines how bail is handled, and the granting of bail depends on factors like the nature of the crime, the risk of flight, and the overall threat to public safety. The decision to grant bail is made by a judge, who will evaluate whether the accused poses a

---

24   https://travel.gc.ca/travelling/advisories/dominican-republic/
      criminal-law-system

significant risk or if there are reasonable conditions under which they can be released pending trial.

In the Dominican Republic, when an individual is arrested, the judge has **up to 48 hours** to decide whether the person can be released on bail. This decision is based on a variety of factors. One of the main considerations is the **seriousness of the offense**. Serious crimes, such as murder, drug trafficking, and organized crime, typically result in bail being **denied**. The judge will also assess the potential flight risk of the individual, especially if the person is a foreign national. If the individual is considered a flight risk or if the crime is particularly severe, bail is less likely to be granted.

If bail is granted, the judge will set an amount that must be paid in order for the individual to be released. This can include a cash deposit, property as collateral, or a guarantee from a third party, known as a surety bond. The judge may also impose conditions on the bail, such as surrendering a passport to prevent the individual from leaving the country, wearing an electronic monitoring bracelet, or regularly reporting to the authorities.

Foreign nationals may face **additional scrutiny** when it comes to bail. Since they do not have permanent ties to the Dominican Republic, they may be considered a higher flight risk. As a result, bail amounts for foreign nationals may be set higher or more stringent conditions may be applied. Additionally, foreign nationals are often required to surrender their passports to ensure they do not leave the country during the legal proceedings. The risk of deportation can also influence decisions about bail. In some cases, if a foreigner is convicted of a serious crime, they may face deportation, which can be a factor in the judge's consideration of bail.

Complaints Against Police

The Dominican Republic's National Police is often seen as the "repressive face of the State." A common sentiment is that the police are

authoritarian, corrupt, and **ineffective.**[25] In 2019, Transparency International's Global Corruption Barometer indicated that the police were among the most corrupt institutions in Latin America and the Caribbean. A 2019 report also revealed that nearly 62 percent of Dominicans believed the police were involved in criminal activities.[26]

Complaints against the police often involve **human rights violations.** These include arbitrary arrests and police violence. There have been reports of the police using excessive force, engaging in racial and class discrimination, and committing unlawful killings. **Corruption** is a significant issue, with police officers sometimes being involved in drug trafficking and arms trafficking.[27] In one instance, a group of National Police officers allegedly stole and sold almost one million rounds of ammunition on the black market (see *Law of the Land True Story* below).

How to File a Complaint Against the Police

If you are a victim of police misconduct in the Dominican Republic, there are several channels available for filing a complaint. First, you can report the issue to the **National Police's Inspector General's Office,** which is responsible for investigating complaints against officers. Complaints can be made in person, by phone, or online through their official website.

Alternatively, you can approach the **Public Prosecutor's Office,** which is responsible for prosecuting crimes, including those committed by police officers. This is especially important if the complaint involves serious offenses, such as **extrajudicial killings** or **torture.** For more serious or complex cases, especially if you feel that your complaint will not be fairly handled by the police, you may seek assistance from **human rights organizations.** These groups can help investigate police misconduct and,

---

25 https://www.france24.com/en/live-news/20220506-police-violence-remains-chronic-struggle-in-dominican-republic

26 https://insightcrime.org/news/brief/police-reform-dominican-republic/

27 https://www.justsecurity.org/109308/
police-network-arms-trafficking-latin-america/

in some cases, provide legal support. Additionally, the **National Human Rights Commission** (*Comisión Nacional de los Derechos Humanos,* or CNDH) is another body you can contact if you believe your human rights have been violated.

There are several organizations in the Dominican Republic that assist with police complaints. The **Comisión Nacional de los Derechos Humanos (CNDH)** helps victims of police abuse and guides them through the legal system. You can reach them via their website or by phone. **The Centro de Estudios de Género (CEG)** focuses on human rights and gender equality, particularly in cases of police violence against women. **The Fundación Pro-Bienestar de la Mujer (PROBIEN)** addresses issues of gender-based violence and can assist those facing police abuse, especially women and marginalized groups. And lastly, **Amnistía Internacional República Dominicana (Amnesty International)** monitors human rights violations, including police misconduct, and offers international support.

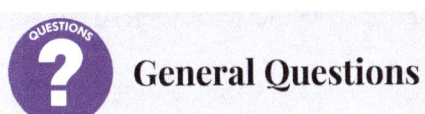

General Questions

1. *If I am convicted in the Dominican Republic, am I likely to be released on bail pending the outcome of my appeal?* In the Dominican Republic, the possibility of being granted bail pending appeal after a conviction depends on various factors. While bail pending appeal is possible, it is generally not guaranteed. The court will assess whether the convicted individual poses a **flight risk** or a **danger to society**, as well as whether the appeal has reasonable chances of success. Bail is more likely to be granted for less serious crimes, while for serious offenses, such as violent crimes or major drug trafficking, it is less common. The judge will also evaluate whether the defendant has ties to the country, the likelihood of them returning for trial, and whether releasing them could undermine the effectiveness of the justice process.

2. ***Who is entitled to bail?*** In the Dominican Republic, bail is generally available to individuals who are arrested for less serious crimes and do not pose a significant risk of fleeing the country or committing further crimes. People facing non-violent offenses, particularly those with strong community ties, are more likely to be eligible for bail. However, individuals charged with serious crimes, such as murder, drug trafficking, or organized crime, are less likely to be granted bail, as the court may determine they are a flight risk or pose a danger to society. The decision to grant bail is ultimately at the discretion of the judge, who will consider the specific circumstances of the case.

3. ***If I am arrested, how soon will I see a judge or magistrate?*** Under Dominican law, if you are arrested, you must be brought before a judge within **48 hours** of your arrest. This is in line with the Criminal Procedure Code, which ensures that the detained person has the right to a judicial review of the arrest. The judge will determine whether there is enough evidence to continue holding you or whether you should be released. This hearing is crucial because it establishes whether the arrest was legal and whether you should remain in custody while awaiting trial or charges.

4. ***Will I be able to contact my country's embassy in the Dominican Republic?*** **Yes.** You are entitled to contact your country's embassy or consulate after being arrested in the Dominican Republic. According to international law and the Vienna Convention on Consular Relations, foreign nationals have the right to notify their embassy or consulate of their arrest. The embassy or consulate can offer assistance in ensuring your rights are respected, provide you with a list of local lawyers, and in some cases, intervene to ensure fair treatment. However, consular officials cannot directly interfere in the legal process, such as preventing your detention or influencing the outcome of a trial.

 **Law of the Land True Story**

In October 2024, Dominican authorities uncovered a corrupt arms trafficking network within the National Police, revealing how deeply arms trafficking and state corruption are intertwined in the region. The network allegedly involved senior officers who stole nearly one million rounds of ammunition and sold them on the black market, some reaching armed gangs in Haiti. This case sheds light on the mechanics of such networks, illustrating how criminal groups profit by exploiting state resources.

The criminal network was led by officers from the National Police's Weapons Superintendency, with key figures including the chief of weapons, his deputy, and an auditor who falsified records. The stolen ammunition was sold through intermediaries, including a civilian who trafficked it to Haitian criminals. Investigations revealed that much of the illicit ammunition came from the Dominican Republic and was smuggled across the border into Haiti, fueling the violence that displaced thousands.

Corruption within government institutions is a significant factor in arms trafficking in Latin America. The Dominican case shows how senior police officers can bypass security measures and falsify records to facilitate illicit sales. This is not unique to the Dominican Republic. Similar networks exist in other countries, such as Colombia, Paraguay, and Brazil, where senior officials use their positions to enable illegal arms trade, sometimes involving front organizations like security firms.

CHAPTER 11
JAILS VS. PRISONS: CONDITIONS & CULTURE

IN THIS CHAPTER

- Overview
- Prison Conditions and Living Environment
- Inmate Rights and Legal Protections
- General Questions

JAILS VS. PRISONS: CONDITIONS & CULTURE

Overview

In the Dominican Republic, as in many other countries, there are key differences between **jails** and **prisons**, both in terms of their functions and the types of individuals they house.

Jails are typically designed for **short-term detention**. They are used to house individuals who are awaiting trial or sentencing or those convicted of **lesser offenses** that carry short sentences. In contrast, prisons are designed for **long-term incarceration** of individuals convicted of more serious crimes and typically serve sentences that extend beyond one year.

The **National Directorate of Prisons** (*Dirección Nacional de Prisiones*) oversees the operation of both jails and prisons in the Dominican Republic. The country has 19 traditional prisons and 22 correctional rehabilitation centers. Traditional prisons have been criticized for overcrowding, abuse, drug trafficking, and extortion. Officially, prisons are managed by a warden, but a military officer often has de facto control. The internal administration and security are entrusted to state security forces like the National Army and the National Police. Many prisons are located in army fortresses and police barracks.[28]

---

28 https://www.cidh.org/countryrep/DominicanRep99/Chapter8.htm

In addition to regular prisons, there are **detention centers** where suspects awaiting trial are held. The conditions of these centers and prisons can vary widely, but **overcrowding** is a significant issue in most facilities. Prisons often have **limited resources**, and conditions can be harsh, with reports of poor sanitation, inadequate medical care, and insufficient food. **Security measures** are varied, with some prisons having higher security levels than others, especially for individuals involved in organized crime or drug trafficking.

The **biggest challenges** in the Dominican Republic's prison system are overcrowding, corruption, poor living conditions, and lack of effective rehabilitation programs. **Overcrowding** is one of the most pressing issues.[29] Prisons and jails often hold more prisoners than they are designed to accommodate, leading to unsanitary conditions and tensions between inmates. **Corruption** within the system also poses a significant challenge, with reports of bribery, mismanagement, and drug trafficking inside the prisons. Additionally, **living conditions** are widespread, with limited access to clean water, healthcare, and basic amenities. These factors contribute to both physical and mental health issues for inmates.

Prison Conditions and Living Environment

In the Dominican Republic, prisons are organized into **different security levels**, but overcrowding often complicates the classification system. **High-security prisons** are designated for individuals convicted of **serious crimes** such as organized crime, drug trafficking, or violent offenses. These facilities are designed to have stricter surveillance, more controlled access, and higher guard-to-inmate ratios. **Medium-security** and **low-security** prisons house individuals convicted of lesser crimes or those serving shorter sentences. However, due to overcrowding, the distinction between these levels is often blurred, and inmates from different categories may be housed together, which can lead to heightened security risks and tensions.

---

29   https://san.com/cc/dominican-republic-prisons-pushed-past-capacity-inmates-held-without-charges/

Access to healthcare in Dominican prisons is **limited** and **substandard**. While larger prisons have basic healthcare facilities, these are often insufficient to meet the needs of the population. Many facilities lack essential medications, equipment, and well-trained medical staff. Serious medical conditions frequently go untreated or are delayed, as the system struggles with inadequate resources. Chronic conditions like HIV, tuberculosis, or mental health disorders are particularly challenging to manage, with few facilities providing proper treatment. Mental healthcare is another neglected area, with many inmates suffering from anxiety, depression, and other disorders due to the harsh conditions. Though some prisons offer psychological support, these services are rare and often unavailable to the majority of prisoners.

Sanitation, food, and **basic needs** in Dominican prisons are also **significant concerns**. The food provided is generally inadequate in both quality and quantity, leaving many prisoners malnourished or relying on support from their families to supplement their diets. The meals are simple and lack nutritional value, which contributes to poor health among inmates. Sanitary conditions in the prisons are poor, with inadequate plumbing, waste disposal, and cleaning facilities. Overcrowding makes these issues worse, as prisoners are forced to share living spaces with limited access to personal hygiene facilities. This leads to unsanitary conditions that can foster the spread of diseases such as gastrointestinal and respiratory illnesses. Basic needs such as clean drinking water, adequate clothing, and personal hygiene products are often lacking, leaving many prisoners unable to maintain basic hygiene, which increases the risk of skin infections and other health problems.

Inmate Rights and Legal Protections

Prisoners in the Dominican Republic retain certain **constitutional rights**, despite their incarceration. The **Constitution of the Dominican Republic** guarantees **basic human rights to all individuals**, including those in prison. These include the **right to life, dignity**, and **protection from cruel or inhumane treatment**. The constitution also ensures the right to be informed of the charges against them and the right to a fair trial. Additionally, inmates are entitled to **access to legal counsel** and have the right to be treated in accordance with international human rights standards.

In terms of **access to legal resources**, prisoners in the Dominican Republic have the right to legal assistance. However, in practice, access to legal support can be limited, especially for those who cannot afford private attorneys. Public defenders are available to assist inmates, but these services are often underfunded, leading to delayed or inadequate legal representation. Moreover, prisoners have the **right to appeal their sentences**, but delays in the judicial system, overcrowded court schedules, and bureaucratic inefficiencies can make it difficult for inmates to fully exercise their right to a fair appeal. The **National Commission for Human Rights** and other legal aid organizations can assist inmates with legal challenges and navigating the appeal process.

Issues of **abuse** in Dominican prisons are a **significant concern**. Inmates often face physical abuse, verbal mistreatment, and neglect from prison staff. **Corruption** within the system, including the smuggling of drugs or weapons, can exacerbate these problems, as guards may turn a blind eye or actively participate in the abuse. Inmates may also suffer from **psychological abuse**, especially in the context of overcrowding and inhumane conditions. Legal recourse for inmates who suffer abuse can be difficult, as the judicial system may not always prioritize the complaints of prisoners, and fear of retaliation by prison staff can deter many inmates from seeking justice. In such cases, organizations like **Amnesty International** and the **National Human Rights Commission** provide support to victims of abuse, helping to document complaints and seek legal recourse through the courts or human rights channels.

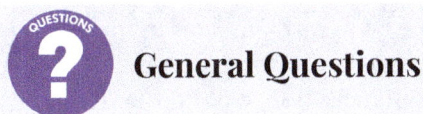 **General Questions**

1. *What is the difference between a jail and prison in the Dominican Republic?* In the Dominican Republic, jails are for short-term detention, housing individuals awaiting trial or serving sentences of under a year. They are typically managed by local authorities and can be overcrowded. Prisons, on the other hand, are for long-term incarceration of those convicted of serious crimes, with sentences longer than one year. Prisons are operated by the national government and have stricter security, housing individuals convicted of more severe offenses like drug trafficking and violent crimes.

2. *Do jails and prisons offer religious services to inmates?* **Yes.** Both jails and prisons in the Dominican Republic generally offer religious services. These services are provided by various religious organizations, including **Catholic** and **Protestant** groups. Inmates can attend regular religious services, Bible studies, and receive spiritual guidance from chaplains or religious volunteers. While availability may vary by facility, religious services are typically part of efforts to support inmate rehabilitation.

3. *How do prisoners spend their time?* Prisoners in the Dominican Republic typically spend their time following a structured daily routine, which includes periods of confinement, work, and limited recreational activities. Most of the day is spent in locked areas, particularly in high-security prisons. However, some facilities offer work programs where inmates can participate in tasks like manual labor, maintenance, or craft workshops. They may also have time for recreational activities, such as sports or socializing with other inmates, although these opportunities can be limited due to overcrowding and lack of resources

4. *What type of jobs can inmates perform?* Inmates in the Dominican Republic can engage in various work programs, including manual labor, maintenance tasks, and production work. Common jobs include cleaning, cooking, and repairing infrastructure like plumbing. Some inmates work in carpentry, sewing, or crafting furniture, which may be sold or used in the prison. Opportunities may also exist for agriculture or construction work. The availability of these jobs depends on the specific prison's resources and policies.

5. *How does the prison commissary system work in the Dominican Republic?* The prison commissary system in the Dominican Republic allows inmates to buy food, toiletries, and other goods with money sent by family or earned through prison work. Commissaries are small shops within prisons, but the selection of items is limited, and prices can be high. Many inmates rely on family support to purchase goods, creating disparities between those with financial backing and those without.

6. *What type of medical care do prisoners receive?* Inmates in the Dominican Republic receive **basic medical care**, but the quality can vary by facility. Prisons typically have in-house medical staff, such as doctors and nurses, to handle common health issues. However, specialized care often requires transfers to external hospitals, which may be delayed. Chronic conditions and serious illnesses are often not adequately addressed, and mental healthcare is limited or lacking in many facilities.

7. *What is prison culture in the Dominican Republic?* Prison culture in the Dominican Republic is marked by overcrowding, violence, and strong gang influence. Inmates often adhere to a hierarchical structure, where those with power control access to food, work, or privileges. Violence between inmates and staff is common, and drug trafficking, extortion, and corruption are widespread. Despite these challenges, some programs aimed at rehabilitation and education exist, though they are often limited in scope and effectiveness.

HELPING A FRIEND OR RELATIVE IMPRISONED IN THE DOMINICAN REPUBLIC

IN THIS CHAPTER

- Overview
- Sending Food, Supplies, and Money to an Inmate
- Mail, Phone Calls, and Visitation
- Prison Scams
- Upon Release

HELPING A FRIEND OR RELATIVE IMPRISONED IN THE DOMINICAN REPUBLIC

Overview

If a family member or friend is imprisoned in the Dominican Republic, it's important to take immediate steps to provide support and ensure their rights are upheld. First, **contact the embassy or consulate** of your home country. They can assist with consular services, including **providing information about the detention** and ensuring that the individual's legal rights are respected. The embassy can also facilitate contact with a **local attorney** and may assist in translating documents or communications if needed. In the Dominican Republic, **U.S. citizens** can contact the **U.S. Embassy in Santo Domingo**, at +(809) 567-7775, or email: SDOAmericans@state.gov. Citizens of other countries should reach out to their respective diplomatic missions.

The **embassy's role** includes ensuring that the individual has access to **legal counsel**, is treated according to international human rights standards, and can communicate with their family. They cannot, however, intervene in the judicial process or provide legal defense. When looking for an **English-speaking attorney**, it's best to ask the embassy for recommendations.

 The U.S. Citizen Services maintains a list of local attorneys in the Dominican Republic, accessible at **https:// do.usembassy.gov/wp-content/uploads/ sites/117/2024/09/List-of-Attorneys-Updated- October-2022-2-2.pdf.**

While not all attorneys in the Dominican Republic speak English, many law firms in larger cities like Santo Domingo may have English-speaking lawyers, particularly those specializing in criminal law or international cases.

Other advice specific to the Dominican Republic includes being prepared for the **bureaucratic process**, which may be slow. Overcrowding in prisons can lead to difficult conditions, so it's important to stay in regular contact with your loved one and the local authorities. Additionally, it's useful to send **funds** to cover necessary expenses like food, toiletries, or legal fees, as the local prison system may not provide for these basic needs. Finally, it is important to be patient and seek support from **human rights organizations** (such as **Amnistía Internacional República Dominicana** and **Comisión Nacional de los Derechos Humanos**), or **local legal aid services** (such as **Public Defenders** or **Legal Assistance Center**) to ensure that your loved one's case is handled fairly.

Sending Food, Supplies, and Money to an Inmate

In the Dominican Republic, family and friends **can bring food** to inmates, but there are **strict regulations** on what can be delivered. Nonperishable food items like packaged snacks, canned goods, and dried foods are typically allowed, while fresh foods such as fruits, meats, or home-cooked meals are usually prohibited for hygiene and security reasons. The specific rules regarding food delivery vary between facilities, so it's important to **check with the prison beforehand**. The food items must be delivered to a designated drop-off area or given directly to the staff and may be inspected.

Sending **packages** to inmates is also allowed, but it is subject to regulations. Permissible items generally include clothing, hygiene products, books, and educational materials. Prohibited items include alcohol, drugs, weapons, electronic devices, and money. Packages will be inspected by prison staff, and any contraband will be confiscated. You should always check the specific guidelines of the prison regarding package contents and procedures.

For sending money, **cash** is usually **not allowed**. Instead, family and friends can use **bank transfers**, **money orders**, or services like **Western Union** or **MoneyGram**. The money is typically deposited into the inmate's account, which can be used to purchase items from the prison commissary. It's important to follow the prison's specific process for money transfers to avoid any issues or delays. Some prisons charge a fee for processing these transactions.

Mail, Phone Calls, and Visitation

Phone Calls

Inmates in the Dominican Republic are **generally not allowed to have cell phones** in prison. Possessing a cell phone is considered illegal, and if found, it can lead to disciplinary action or extended sentences. However, **inmates may still be able to make and receive calls**, though this typically takes place through **prison-controlled phone systems**.

Most prisons have **designated phone areas** where inmates can make calls, usually to family members or legal counsel. The calls are often **limited in duration**, and the inmate's access to a phone may be restricted to certain hours. Calls are typically made **collect** or through a **prepaid system**, where the inmate's family or friends deposit money into an account to fund the calls.

There are no uniform policies across all prisons in the country, and **phone access can vary significantly**, depending on the facility's security level, resources, and regulations. In some prisons, access to phones might be more restricted, while others may offer more frequent access during designated times. Additionally, phone calls may be **monitored** for security reasons.

It's important to check with the specific prison for their policies on phone use, as rules and availability may change based on location and current conditions within the facility.

Visiting

Visitation in Dominican prisons is **allowed under strict rules**. Family members, close friends, and legal representatives are typically permitted to visit inmates, though special permission may be required for others. The frequency of visits varies by facility, but inmates are usually allowed visits once or twice a week, depending on the prison's policies and security level.

Visitors must present identification, such as a national ID or passport, and may undergo a security screening, which could include searches of personal belongings. Food, money, and other items are generally not allowed unless authorized by prison authorities. Visitors should arrive on time and adhere to the designated visiting hours, which are set in advance.

Prisons typically have designated areas for visits, like visiting rooms or outdoor spaces. Physical contact is often limited, with only minimal contact, such as a handshake, permitted. Visits are usually monitored by security staff to ensure safety.

Important things to know include adhering to a modest dress code, preparing for security checks, and bringing proper identification. Visitors must also respect visitation hours and understand what items can or cannot be brought into the facility. Since each prison may have specific rules, it's important to contact the facility ahead of time to confirm details.

Prison Scams

In the Dominican Republic, as in many other countries, prison scams do exist. These scams can target the families and friends of prisoners, taking advantage of their emotions or their desire to help their loved ones. Some common scams involve individuals pretending to be prison officials, lawyers, or even the inmates themselves. Scammers may claim that an inmate requires money for bail, medical treatment, or legal assistance. They often use high-pressure tactics to convince victims to send money quickly, either via bank transfers, money orders, or other methods.

One of the most common red flags to watch out for is **unsolicited communication**, particularly from unknown phone numbers or individuals claiming to represent the prison. If you are contacted by someone claiming that your relative or friend in prison urgently needs money or legal help, be cautious. Another red flag is **requests for payment via untraceable methods**, such as wire transfers to personal accounts or the use of third-party intermediaries. If someone pressures you to act quickly, especially without providing clear documentation or official channels for payment, it's a warning sign that the situation may not be legitimate.

If you think you're being scammed, the first thing to do is **stop communication immediately** and **do not send any money or provide personal information**. Contact the prison directly using the official contact details to verify the information. If you are still unsure, seek the help of a trusted lawyer or contact your embassy for guidance. Additionally, you can **report the incident to local authorities**, such as the National Police or a consumer protection agency, who may investigate the scam. It's important to remember that legitimate requests for help will typically go through official channels and will provide clear documentation.

Upon Release

Upon release from prison or jail in the Dominican Republic, foreigners may face additional legal obligations or restrictions. In general, once an inmate completes their sentence or is granted parole, they are allowed to leave the country. However, **foreign nationals** may be subject to specific conditions, such as **immigration checks** or **deportation** procedures. If the individual was arrested for violating immigration laws or overstaying their visa, they could be **deported** immediately after serving their sentence, depending on the circumstances and the decisions made by immigration authorities.

Some foreigners may also face **restrictions on re-entry** to the Dominican Republic or other countries, depending on the nature of their offense. If their criminal record is flagged, it could impact their ability to travel freely or enter certain countries. Additionally, some foreign nationals might be placed under **supervision** after release, particularly if they are required to report to immigration or local authorities regularly.

While there are no universal post-release rules, foreign prisoners should also be aware of their **right to appeal or challenge any post-release conditions.** If a foreign national has been convicted of a serious crime, they might have to comply with **special regulations** or restrictions, including monitoring or reporting to law enforcement or other government agencies.

It's important for released individuals to consult with legal counsel, especially if they are unsure of their status or future legal obligations after release. This ensures that they comply with any remaining legal requirements, avoiding further legal issues or complications.

THE ADMINISTRATION OF JUSTICE

IN THIS CHAPTER

- Dominican Legal System
- General Questions
- Law of the Land True Story
- Takeaways

THE ADMINISTRATION OF JUSTICE

Dominican Legal System[30]

The Dominican Republic's legal system is rooted in the **civil law tradition**, which has its origins in Roman law. The legal framework was influenced by the **French Napoleonic Code** and the legal systems of Spain, from which the country gained independence. Key components of the Dominican legal system include **the Constitution**, which serves as the supreme law of the land, **civil law codes**, and various **laws** passed by the National Congress. The legal system is based on the principle of **separation of powers**, with the judiciary acting independently from the executive and legislative branches.

The judiciary is structured around several levels of courts. The **Supreme Court of Justice** is the highest judicial body, serving as the final court of appeal for cases. Beneath it are **Appellate Courts**, which hear appeals from lower courts, and **First Instance Courts**, which handle the majority of civil, criminal, and administrative cases. **Specialized courts** exist for family law, labor disputes, and electoral issues. Additionally, there are **tribunals** for specific matters, such as **military courts** and **constitutional courts**.

---

30 https://www.nyulawglobal.org/globalex/dominican_republic.html

One distinctive feature of the Dominican judiciary is its **focus on legal formality**, as it is largely based on written legal codes rather than case law or judicial precedent, as seen in common law systems. This sometimes leads to a reliance on rigid interpretation of the law, which may not always account for changing societal dynamics. The judiciary is also **centralized**, with all courts operating under the jurisdiction of the Supreme Court.

Despite its robust structure, the Dominican judicial system faces several challenges. **Corruption** within the judiciary is a major issue, with allegations of bribery and influence-peddling affecting the outcomes of some cases. Additionally, there are concerns about **delays in the judicial process** and **backlogs** in the courts, leading to prolonged waiting times for cases to be resolved. **Lack of resources** and insufficient funding also hamper the efficiency of the judicial system, limiting access to justice, especially for marginalized communities. Efforts are being made to reform and modernize the judiciary, but progress has been slow, and these challenges continue to affect public trust in the system.

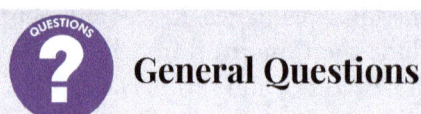 **General Questions**

1. *Will the court treat first-time offenders and tourists with more leniency?* The court may show some leniency to first-time offenders, particularly if the offense is minor or if the individual demonstrates remorse or cooperation. However, the treatment of first-time offenders in the Dominican Republic is generally dependent on the nature of the crime committed and the judge's discretion. Tourists may not necessarily receive more leniency simply because of their foreign status, as the law applies equally to locals and foreigners. However, the circumstances of their case, such as the lack of criminal intent or misunderstandings due to cultural differences, may be taken into account.

2. ***If I am charged with a crime, which court is likely to hear my case?*** If you are charged with a crime in the Dominican Republic, the case is most likely to be heard in a **First Instance Court** (*Tribunal de Primera Instancia*). These courts handle the majority of criminal cases, including both felonies and misdemeanors. The specific court within this category will depend on the nature of the crime and its severity. For more serious or complex cases, the matter may be escalated to an **Appellate Court** or, in exceptional cases, a **Specialized Court** (e.g., for organized crime or drug trafficking).

3. ***What is the standard of proof in a criminal case in the Dominican Republic?*** In criminal cases in the Dominican Republic, the standard of proof is typically **"beyond a reasonable doubt"** (*más allá de toda duda razonable*). This means that the prosecution must provide sufficient evidence to convince the judge or court that the accused is guilty, without leaving any reasonable doubts about their innocence.

 **Law of the Land True Story**[31]

In November 2015, the Dominican Republic's judiciary faced intense scrutiny following the suspension of five judges implicated in a case-fixing scandal. Attorney General Francisco Dominguez Brito revealed that further investigations could involve more judges, as suspicions of widespread irregularities within the judicial system mounted. The Judiciary Council moved swiftly, suspending Judges Jose Duverge Mejia, Roso Vallejo Espinosa, Victor Mejia Lebron, Awilda Reyes Beltre, and Delio German Figueroa from their positions.

---

31 https://www.sandiegouniontribune.com/2015/11/17/ dominican-judges-investigated-amid-suspicions-of-corruption/

This scandal centered around allegations that a law office, purportedly operated by former Judiciary Council member Francisco Arias Valera, had manipulated cases linked to organized crime, including drug trafficking, money laundering, and corruption. Arias Valera allegedly used large bribes to influence Judge Reyes Beltre, pressuring her to issue favorable rulings, such as the controversial release of accused murderer Erinson de los Santos Solis.

This event underscored deep concerns about corruption and the integrity of the Dominican Republic's judicial system. The Attorney General emphasized that the investigation would go further, signaling a commitment to addressing systemic corruption that undermined public trust in the judiciary. This case became a key turning point in discussions about the need for judicial reform and greater transparency within the Dominican Republic.

 **Takeaways**

- The Dominican Republic's legal system is based on civil law, influenced by the French Napoleonic Code and Spanish traditions. It relies on written legal codes rather than case law, with the Supreme Court as the highest authority.

- The Dominican legal system is designed around the separation of powers, with the judiciary intended to function independently from the executive and legislative branches. However, in practice, the system's independence has been compromised by corruption and political influence, affecting judicial decisions.

- The Dominican judicial system's reliance on rigid written codes, rather than case law or judicial precedent, can sometimes hinder its ability to adapt to changing societal dynamics. This legal formalism may not always address contemporary issues effectively, potentially leading to injustices or outdated interpretations of the law.

- In criminal cases, the standard of proof in the Dominican Republic is "beyond a reasonable doubt" (*más allá de toda duda razonable*). This means the prosecution must present sufficient evidence to convince the judge that the accused is guilty without leaving any reasonable doubts.

- The system faces issues such as corruption, bribery, and inefficiencies, leading to questionable case outcomes and delays. Insufficient resources hinder access to justice, especially for marginalized groups.

CRIME VICTIM ASSISTANCE

IN THIS CHAPTER

- Overview
- What to Do If You Are the Victim of a Crime
- Common Tourist Scams in the Dominican Republic
- Sexual Assault
- Consular Assistance
- General Questions

CHAPTER 14
CRIME VICTIM ASSISTANCE

Overview

Crime victims in the Dominican Republic have access to various **support services**, both from **government agencies** and **non-governmental organizations** (NGOs), which help them cope with the aftermath of criminal acts. These resources range from legal assistance and psychological support to emergency services and social aid.

The government provides several services aimed at assisting victims. **The National Police** (*Policía Nacional*) is the **primary law enforcement agency** responsible for responding to crimes and offering protection. Within the National Police, the **Victim Assistance Unit** (*Unidad de Atención a la Víctima - UAV*) provides emotional support and guides victims through the legal process. The **Public Prosecutor's Office** (*Ministerio Público*) handles the prosecution of criminal cases and helps victims navigate the judicial system. There is also a specialized **Domestic Violence Unit** within the Public Prosecutor's Office that focuses on cases of gender-based violence, sexual assault, and domestic abuse. **The Ministry of Women** (*Ministerio de la Mujer*) addresses the specific needs of women victims of domestic violence and sexual assault, providing shelters, psychological counseling, and legal assistance. Additionally, the **National Institute of Forensic Sciences** (INACIF) provides forensic services, such as autopsies and other medical examinations, crucial for criminal investigations. The Dominican government also offers **social support programs** for victims of crime, which may include financial aid, housing assistance, and access to healthcare. These programs aim to help victims recover from their immediate needs and regain stability.

In addition to government resources, numerous **NGOs** provide **vital services to crime victims**. Organizations like the **Fundación de Mujeres en Desarrollo** (FUMD) focus on supporting women who have experienced domestic violence and sexual assault by offering legal aid, psychological counseling, and emergency shelter. The **Centro de Estudios de Género** (CEG) also assists women by providing legal support and advocacy for gender equality. The **Red de Defensa de los Derechos Humanos** (RDDH) helps individuals who have faced human rights abuses, offering legal support and advocacy. The **Fundación de Ayuda a Víctimas de Violencia** (FAVI) is another key NGO, providing medical attention, legal aid, and psychological support to women and children who are victims of violence. The **Centro de Apoyo a la Mujer** (CAM) works to help women reintegrate into society after experiencing violence by providing counseling, legal assistance, and rehabilitation services.

For emergency situations, crime victims can contact the **national emergency number 911**, which connects them with police, medical teams, and other first responders. Victims of crime can also directly reach the National Police at 809-200-3673 for assistance or to report a crime. The Ministry of Women operates a specific **hotline for victims of domestic violence and sexual assault**, which can be reached at **809-540-0080**. Victims in need of medical attention can call the same emergency number (911) or contact local hospitals directly for immediate care.

The Dominican Republic also offers specialized services for sexual violence and domestic abuse victims, particularly through organizations like **UNICEF**, which partners with local agencies to provide safe spaces, hotline services, and support for children and women. Various legal aid services are available, often through NGOs, to ensure that low-income victims have access to justice. Psychological support is also readily available through both government entities and local NGOs, with many offering free or low-cost therapy to help victims process trauma and rebuild their lives.

Visitors who have been victims of crime and wish to pursue legal action can access legal assistance through various means. While the Dominican Republic does not have a public legal assistance system for **foreign nationals** specifically, certain **NGOs** can provide legal counseling, especially in cases of serious crimes. The **Prosecutor's Office** (*Ministerio Público*) can also provide assistance to foreigners, and victims may opt to hire a local attorney to represent them through the judicial process.

What to Do If You Are the Victim of a Crime

If you become a victim of a crime in the Dominican Republic, your first priority should be ensuring your safety. If you are in immediate danger, move to a secure location, such as a public space, and call the emergency services number **911**, which connects to police, medical, and fire services. If necessary, also contact the **National Police** at **809-200-3673** or reach out to the **Tourist Police** at **809-200-3500**, who specialize in assisting foreign visitors. Once you are in a safe place, it's important to report the crime to the authorities by visiting the nearest police station to file a formal report. Request a **police report** (*denuncia*), as this will be essential for any legal actions, insurance claims, or support from your embassy.

After ensuring that the crime is reported, seek medical attention if you have been injured, whether it's immediately after the incident or if you feel unwell later. Emergency medical services can be reached via **911**, or you can go directly to a nearby hospital. It's also crucial to **contact your embassy or consulate**. They can help you navigate the local legal system, provide translation services, offer guidance on next steps, and assist with any additional resources, such as finding legal representation.

In addition to medical and legal support, it's important to **document everything related to the crime**, including the police report, medical records, photographs of injuries or damages, and any other relevant details. Your embassy can help you with translating documents and connecting with local legal services if needed. If the crime involves serious injury or trauma, you might want to consider seeking **psychological support**, either from local services or organizations that specialize in trauma counseling. Keep in mind that reporting the crime, staying in contact with authorities, and following up on investigations are key steps in ensuring your safety and receiving appropriate support during your recovery process.

Common Tourist Scams in the Dominican Republic

Tourists in the Dominican Republic can be vulnerable to a **variety of scams**, with some of the most common involving overcharging, fake tour operators, and street vendors. One common scam is when tourists are approached by street vendors or taxi drivers who offer seemingly great deals on goods, services, or tours, only to charge **inflated prices** or deliver **subpar services**. Another scam involves "friendly" locals offering to guide tourists or provide information, but then insisting on **exorbitant tips or fees** once the service is rendered. In tourist hotspots, **counterfeit** or **overpriced excursions** are also a concern, where travelers might pay for activities or tours that don't exist or are far less impressive than advertised.

Another common scam targeting tourists in the Dominican Republic is the **"credit card skimming"** scheme, where fraudsters use hidden devices to steal card information at ATMs or in shops. Tourists should always use ATMs located in well-lit, secure areas, preferably inside banks or hotel lobbies, and avoid withdrawing large sums of cash at once.

To avoid these scams, it's essential to **stay vigilant** and recognize the red flags. Always use **official taxis or ride-sharing** services like Uber, as unauthorized drivers often overcharge. When booking excursions or tours, only go through **reputable, licensed operators** or your hotel's concierge service, and ensure the details of the service are clear before agreeing to any payment. Avoid accepting unsolicited offers from strangers on the street, especially when they seem too eager to help or provide services. Also, agree on **prices upfront** when dealing with vendors, whether it's for transportation, souvenirs, or food. By exercising caution and staying informed, tourists can significantly reduce their chances of falling victim to scams during their stay.

Verify the prices of drinks or services before accepting offers. Being cautious, asking for clarity on prices and terms, and sticking to trusted establishments can help protect tourists from falling victim to these common scams.

Sexual Assault

Once in a safe place, it is imperative you report the assault at the nearest police station. It's important to file a **police report** (*denuncia*) that includes all relevant details about the incident. The police will guide you through the next steps, including gathering evidence and beginning the investigation. If language is a barrier, officers can assist with translation services.

As a victim of sexual assault in the Dominican Republic, you have several important rights. You are entitled to **free medical care**, including forensic exams, which are crucial for documenting injuries and collecting evidence. You can also request **psychological support** to help you process the trauma of the assault, and there are organizations like the **Victim Assistance Unit** of the National Police or local NGOs that offer services. Additionally, you have the **right to legal representation**. If you cannot afford an attorney, you can request free legal aid. Your embassy or consulate can provide additional support, including connecting you with local attorneys or helping you navigate the legal system in a foreign country.

It is also important to follow **safety recommendations** after the assault. Seek medical care as soon as possible to receive appropriate treatment and to ensure that evidence is collected, which may be critical for prosecution. Avoid showering, changing clothes, or brushing your teeth before you receive a forensic exam, as it can affect the collection of evidence. Your embassy will be a valuable resource for guidance and can help with emotional and legal support, such as referring you to trusted professionals or local organizations dedicated to helping survivors of sexual violence. Stay in well-populated areas and use official taxis or ride-sharing services to minimize risk during your stay.

Sexual assault is a serious crime, and you have the right to receive support, respect, and justice in the Dominican Republic. Reporting the crime and accessing medical and legal assistance are important steps toward recovery and ensuring accountability for the perpetrator.

Consular Assistance

If you become a victim of a crime in the Dominican Republic, your embassy or consulate can offer crucial support. They can assist in navigating the local legal system, help you report the crime, and provide a safe space to contact family or friends. Embassies can offer **a list of reputable local lawyers** if you need legal representation and can sometimes assist with language barriers by providing translation services. They can also help with the replacement of lost or stolen passports, arrange emergency travel documents, and provide information on local medical facilities if you need immediate treatment.

However, it's important to note that consular assistance has **limitations**. While they can provide guidance and connect you with resources, they cannot intervene directly in local legal matters or provide financial assistance for legal fees or medical costs. They also cannot act as your legal representative or investigate the crime on your behalf. Consulates do not have the authority to compel local authorities to take specific actions, and they cannot assist in civil matters such as personal disputes or financial issues related to the crime. Their role is primarily focused on ensuring your safety, helping with essential services, and guiding you through the process.

 **General Questions**

1. *If I am a victim of a crime, can I legally be compensated?* In the Dominican Republic, victims of violent crimes may pursue compensation through the judicial system by filing a civil lawsuit against the perpetrator, but this depends on the assailant's apprehension and conviction. While there are limited government programs for crime victims, especially in cases of assault or sexual violence, compensation is not always guaranteed. Tourists with insurance may also be eligible for compensation through their provider for medical expenses or property loss, though legal compensation can be a lengthy process.

2. *If a family member falls victim to homicide, can I bring the body back to my home country?* **Yes**. You can repatriate a body if a family member is a homicide victim in the Dominican Republic. After the police and forensic authorities release the body, you will need a **death certificate** and may require embalming and a **mortuary certificate** for transport. Your embassy can assist with the documentation and connect you to repatriation services. You must also comply with your home country's customs and health regulations, which may include permits and fees for transportation.

3. *How does the Dominican Republic handle the protection of witnesses and victims during criminal trials?* The Dominican Republic has measures in place to protect witnesses and victims during criminal trials, although the effectiveness can vary. The National Police and Public Ministry are responsible for ensuring safety, and in serious cases like organized crime or violent offenses, witness protection programs may include relocation or changes in identity. Victims of crimes, particularly in cases of domestic violence or sexual assault, can access Victim Assistance Units within the National Police, which offer emotional support and guidance through the legal process. While legal protections, such as confidentiality, exist, the country's ability to fully safeguard witnesses and victims may be limited by resources, though efforts to improve these protections are ongoing.

CHAPTER 15

POLICE

IN THIS CHAPTER

- Overview
- Police Response
- Police and Community Relations
- Police Use of Force
- Law of the Land True Story

CHAPTER 15

POLICE

Overview

The police in the Dominican Republic is organized into several branches, each responsible for different aspects of law enforcement. **The primary national police force** is the **National Police** (*Policía Nacional*), which is responsible for maintaining general public order, investigating crimes, and ensuring the safety of citizens across the country. The National Police operates at the national level, overseeing most law enforcement activities. There is also a specialized **Tourist Police** (*Policía Turística*) dedicated to assisting foreign visitors in tourist areas, ensuring their safety and addressing issues that may arise for tourists. Additionally, some municipalities have local **municipal police** forces, which focus on enforcing local ordinances, traffic laws, and maintaining order within city limits, though their authority is limited compared to the National Police.

The Dominican Republic's police force is relatively large, with approximately **40,000 active officers** serving across various divisions and units. While this number may seem adequate for a country with a population of around 11 million, there are concerns about whether the force is properly staffed and equipped to handle the country's crime rates and growing security challenges. There are often criticisms that the police force is understaffed in certain regions, and the force faces challenges in terms of training, resources, and equipment. Police officers sometimes lack sufficient support to deal effectively with organized crime, drug trafficking, and high crime rates in urban areas. The Dominican government continues to implement reforms and seek international cooperation to improve police efficiency and accountability, but staffing and resource issues remain a concern in fully addressing the country's security needs.

Police Response

The police response in the Dominican Republic is primarily focused on maintaining public safety, enforcing laws, and responding to criminal activity. The key functions of the **National Police** (*Policía Nacional*) include patrolling urban and rural areas, responding to emergencies, conducting criminal investigations, managing traffic, and ensuring public order. Specialized units, such as the **Tourist Police** (*Policía Turística*), are deployed to safeguard foreign visitors and handle incidents in popular tourist areas, while the **Criminal Investigations Department** (*Dirección Central de Investigación*) focuses on major crimes like homicide, organized crime, and drug trafficking. The **Traffic Police** is responsible for regulating road safety and traffic-related offenses, while **Specialized Anti-Narcotics Units** address drug-related crimes.

However, the Dominican Republic's police force faces several challenges, particularly concerning **crime rates, resource shortages**, and **public trust**. Despite having a relatively large police force, the country struggles with inadequate training, outdated equipment, and insufficient funding, which hinders the police's ability to effectively combat high rates of violent crime, drug trafficking, and organized criminal networks. There is also a lack of coordination between various branches of the police, leading to inefficiencies in operations. Furthermore, corruption and allegations of police misconduct have eroded public trust in law enforcement, making cooperation from the community difficult.

In response to these challenges, the Dominican government has initiated a range of **police reforms** aimed at improving efficiency and public confidence. These reforms include efforts to enhance police training, better equip officers with modern technology, and promote transparency within the force. Notable reforms have focused on **community**

policing, which aims to build trust between the police and local communities, and **police accountability** measures designed to reduce corruption and misconduct. The government has also collaborated with international organizations and foreign governments to strengthen its law enforcement capabilities, particularly in the fight against organized crime and narcotrafficking. Despite these efforts, significant challenges remain, and much work is still needed to address the structural issues within the police force and improve overall security in the country.

Police and Community Relations

The overall image and perception of the police in the Dominican Republic is **mixed**, with many citizens and visitors holding concerns about corruption, inefficiency, and abuse of power. While the police are generally seen as the institution responsible for maintaining public order and safety, **public trust** in law enforcement is **often low**, especially in urban areas. Allegations of **corruption**, **bribery**, and **police misconduct** are widespread, and there are frequent reports of abuse of power, including excessive use of force and involvement in criminal activities such as drug trafficking. This has led to a perception that some officers may not be fully committed to protecting the public or upholding the law.

Additionally, the police's ability to effectively combat rising crime rates, particularly in high-crime areas, is often questioned. Many people feel that the police are not adequately equipped, trained, or supported to deal with the country's security challenges, such as gang violence and organized crime. This has created a sense of frustration among the population, leading some to view the police force as ineffective or even corrupt.

However, there are also efforts to improve the police force's image. Recent reforms, such as increased police transparency, better training, and a focus on **community policing**, aim to rebuild trust between the police and the public. The **Tourist Police** (*Policía Turística*) has a somewhat better reputation among visitors, as it is seen as more professional and helpful in addressing concerns specific to tourists. Despite these efforts, the overall perception remains somewhat negative, with many citizens and observers calling for deeper reforms to address systemic issues within the police force.

Police Use of Force

Police use of force is a significant issue in the Dominican Republic, and it has been a point of concern for both citizens and human rights organizations. There have been multiple reports of excessive use of force by police officers, particularly during routine arrests, protests, and encounters with individuals from marginalized communities. Instances of **brutality, unnecessary violence**, and **fatal shootings** have been documented, leading to growing public criticism. This problem is exacerbated by a lack of proper training on de-escalation tactics and a culture that sometimes tolerates abuse, contributing to a broader erosion of public trust in law enforcement.

One of the key areas of concern is the **use of firearms** by police officers, particularly in situations where they could have used non-lethal force. In many cases, people have been killed or severely injured during arrests or confrontations that could have been handled differently. For example, **protests** and demonstrations have occasionally escalated when police used force against demonstrators, raising concerns about the abuse of power. This issue is especially pronounced in poorer urban neighborhoods, where tensions between the police and the public are higher, leading to perceptions of abuse and discrimination.

 **Law of the Land True Story**[32]

In 2022, a tragic incident in the Dominican Republic drew attention to the ongoing problem of police violence. David de los Santos, a 24-year-old man, was arrested after a minor argument with a store clerk at a shopping mall in Santo Domingo. Just three days later, he died from head trauma while in police custody. The official police report claimed that de los Santos had suffered a nervous breakdown and caused his own injuries. However, an autopsy revealed that he

---

32   https://www.france24.com/en/live-news/20220506-police-violence-remains-chronic-struggle-in-dominican-republic

had been killed, and his family accused the police of torture, including allegations of severe physical abuse.

This case sparked public outrage, especially as it was not an isolated incident. The death of de los Santos was the third police-related killing in just a few weeks, further highlighting the widespread issue of police brutality in the country. Protests erupted in the streets, with citizens demanding justice and calling attention to the systemic violence that disproportionately affects poor and marginalized communities. Human rights organizations have long pointed to the role that racial and economic factors play in how people are treated by law enforcement. They argue that those from poorer backgrounds, like de los Santos, are more likely to suffer from police violence.

Despite promises of reform from the government, including the sacking of police officials and pledges for better training, incidents of excessive force continue to occur. In fact, just weeks before de los Santos's death, another man, Jose Gregorio Custodio, died after being tortured by police. These cases are part of a troubling pattern of violence, with more than 4,000 deaths recorded in police clashes over the past decade. The response from authorities has often been to deny any wrongdoing, but the public remains skeptical of the police's commitment to addressing these issues. The tragic death of de los Santos and the ongoing cycle of police violence serve as a stark reminder of the need for significant reform in the Dominican Republic's police force.

HOW TO GET LEGAL HELP IN THE DOMINICAN REPUBLIC

IN THIS CHAPTER

- Available Resources
- Legal Aid
- Foreign Embassies in the Dominican Republic

HOW TO GET LEGAL HELP IN THE DOMINICAN REPUBLIC

Available Resources

To find reliable legal representation in the Dominican Republic, begin by identifying your specific legal needs and then seek a **reputable law firm or practitioner**. It is important to hire a lawyer familiar with Dominican law, culture, and language. You can find lawyers through referrals, online platforms, or law firm directories. Before hiring a lawyer, make sure there are clear agreements on billing, total costs, and the lawyer's responsibilities.

 The **Dominican Bar Association** is an excellent resource for finding qualified legal professionals; to learn more, visit **https://www.dominicanbarassociation.org/**.

 Embassies also maintain **lists of local attorneys** in the Dominican Republic, providing helpful guidelines on how to select one. For example, the U.S. Embassy list can be found at **https://do.usembassy.gov/wp-content/uploads/sites/117/2024/09/List-of-Attorneys-Updated-October-2022-2-2.pdf**.

Bear in mind that the Department of State assumes no responsibility or liability for the professional ability, reputation, or quality of services provided by the individuals on this list and inclusion on the list is not an endorsement by the Department or the U.S. government. Contact several attorneys to briefly describe the services you need and inquire about their qualifications and experience. You can verify a lawyer's credentials by requesting proof of qualification and checking with the Dominican Bar Association.

In addition to seeking legal counsel, if you're facing an arrest or are detained in the Dominican Republic, there are emergency assistance organizations that can provide support. **The Dominican Red Cross** (*Cruz Roja Dominicana*) offers emergency medical assistance and can be contacted if you're injured during an arrest or detention. The **National Commission on Human Rights** (**CNDH**) is another important resource, providing advocacy and legal advice for those whose rights have been violated by authorities.

For immediate emergency situations, such as a wrongful arrest or an urgent need for legal help, you can also contact the **National Police** directly at their emergency number **911** for assistance. If you're in need of protection or feel threatened, the **Tourist Police** (*Policía Turística*) may also be able to help, especially if you're a foreigner facing legal issues in tourist areas. Having these resources at your disposal can ensure that you receive the proper support and legal advice in case of an arrest in the Dominican Republic.

Legal Aid

Foreign visitors in the Dominican Republic can access legal aid, but their eligibility is subject to **certain conditions** and **limitations**. The **Public Defender's Office** (*Defensoría Pública*) provides legal assistance primarily to individuals who cannot afford to hire a private lawyer. While this service is mostly directed at Dominican citizens, foreign visitors in a similar financial position may also be eligible, especially if they face serious legal issues, such as criminal charges, detention, or violations of their basic rights.

The **process** for accessing legal aid as a foreigner typically involves demonstrating **financial need**—proof that the individual cannot afford legal representation. Visitors would need to submit **relevant documentation**, which may include evidence of income or lack of financial resources, to qualify for assistance. In some cases, a **consulate or embassy** may also provide support in facilitating access to legal aid or helping navigate the legal system in the country. While the process can be straightforward for those with limited resources, it may be more complex for tourists or expatriates unfamiliar with the Dominican legal system.

The **criteria** for receiving legal aid are based on two main factors: the **economic status** of the individual and the **nature of the case**. The Public Defender's Office prioritizes those who cannot afford a private attorney, and legal aid is generally reserved for **criminal cases**—such as those involving arrests, charges, or imprisonment. However, some cases involving **family law** issues (like custody or divorce) or **civil rights violations** may also be eligible for legal assistance, particularly if they involve an injustice or violation of the individual's rights.

What **legal aid encompasses** includes **representation in criminal cases**, such as defense during trials, consultation with a public defender, and assistance with legal documentation. Legal aid may also cover **interviews with law enforcement** or prosecutors, helping individuals navigate the legal procedures involved in their case. However, the scope of this assistance can be limited. For example, legal aid typically **does not cover appeals** or cases that fall outside the criminal justice system, such as **complex civil suits** or **corporate disputes**, unless the case involves significant violation of rights or extreme economic hardship. In such instances, visitors may need to seek private legal counsel for further legal actions.

It's also important to note that the quality and availability of legal aid may vary depending on the specific region or area in the Dominican Republic. In major cities like Santo Domingo, where legal infrastructure is more developed, foreign visitors may have more access to qualified public defenders. However, in rural or less-populated areas, the availability of such services could be limited. Therefore, while legal aid exists for those who qualify, foreign visitors may still find it **beneficial to seek private attorneys** for more comprehensive legal representation.

Foreign Embassies in the Dominican Republic

Foreign embassies and consulates in the Dominican Republic play a vital role in assisting their citizens with a variety of consular services. These services include providing **legal assistance**, issuing **emergency travel documents**, offering **assistance during crises** or emergencies, and **facilitating communication** between the individual and their home country's government. In cases of arrests, detentions, or legal disputes, embassies and consulates can help by offering **lists of local attorneys**, guiding citizens through the legal system, and offering **advice on local laws and regulations**. Embassies also work to ensure the safety of their citizens and advocate for their rights in situations of **injustice** or **discrimination**.

Embassies and consulates are typically located in the country's **capital**, with the **Santo Domingo** area being the central hub for foreign diplomatic missions. While most embassies are situated in or near the capital city, there are also consulates in other key regions and cities, such as **Puerto Plata** and **Santiago**, to ensure broader coverage and support for foreign nationals across the Dominican Republic. The capital, Santo Domingo, hosts most of the **main embassies**, while **consulates** in other cities serve to address the needs of citizens living outside the capital.

For **U.S. citizens** in the Dominican Republic, the U.S. has one of the most prominent diplomatic missions in the country. The **U.S. Embassy** is located in **Santo Domingo**, which serves as the main hub for **visa processing, emergency assistance**, and **consular services**. Additionally, the **U.S. Consular Agency** in **Puerto Plata** provides support to American citizens living or visiting in that region. U.S. consulates and agencies also exist in other parts of the country, helping to manage services for American nationals in the Dominican Republic, including in regions with significant tourist populations.

These diplomatic missions are crucial for ensuring that U.S. citizens have the support they need while in the Dominican Republic, whether it's related to passport issues, emergency assistance, legal problems, or general guidance on navigating life in a foreign country.

MEDICAL FACILITIES & HOSPITALS

IN THIS CHAPTER

- Overview
- Visitors' Access to Healthcare in the Dominican Republic
- Dominican Hospitals
- General Questions
- Insurance Guidance

MEDICAL FACILITIES & HOSPITALS

Overview[33]

The healthcare system in the Dominican Republic has made significant strides in recent years, particularly in urban areas like **Santo Domingo**, where hospitals and medical facilities offer a relatively high standard of care. The country's healthcare system is a mix of **public** and **private** services. The **public healthcare system** provides basic services through government-run hospitals and clinics, which are generally more afford-able but can suffer from limited resources, long waiting times, and over-crowding. On the other hand, **private hospitals and clinics** tend to offer higher quality care, more modern equipment, and shorter wait times, though they are often more expensive.

The public healthcare system is managed by the **Ministry of Public Health** (*Ministerio de Salud Pública*) and provides services to the ma-jority of the population, including basic care, emergency services, and public health programs. The **private sector** caters to those who can af-ford to pay out-of-pocket or have private health insurance. **Health in-surance** is common among many residents, and foreigners who are stay-ing in the country for extended periods may also opt for **private health insurance plans** for better coverage.

---

33 https://dreamingdr.com/healthcare-insurance-dominican-republic/

For **foreign visitors**, the accessibility, quality, and affordability of medical services vary. Private healthcare facilities are often preferred by tourists, expatriates, and those seeking specialized treatment. **Emergency medical services** are generally reliable in larger cities, but the quality of care may be lower in rural areas or less-developed regions. Visitors should be aware that while healthcare is generally affordable compared to many Western countries, **medical costs** can still be high at private hospitals and clinics, especially for services like **emergency surgery** or **specialized treatment**. It's recommended that travelers have **travel insurance** that includes **medical evacuation** and **emergency services** to avoid unexpected high costs.

In terms of emergency services, the **Dominican Republic** has a **national emergency number, 911**, which connects callers to **ambulance services**, **fire departments**, and **police**. This number is available in most urban areas, but services may be less reliable or slower in remote areas. For **non-emergency medical concerns**, visitors can seek assistance from private clinics or pharmacies, which are widely available across the country. It's also important for visitors to keep contact information for their embassy or consulate in case they need assistance in accessing medical services or navigating a medical emergency.

Visitors' Access to Healthcare in the Dominican Republic[34]

Healthcare services in the Dominican Republic for visitors are accessible through private health insurance or out-of-pocket payments, particularly in **tourist areas** where quality care is available. However, **language barriers** can pose challenges, as Spanish is the primary language spoken. Visitors should have **adequate health insurance** or be prepared to pay upfront for medical services, as many hospitals require **cash payment before treatment**. In tourist areas, private clinics and hospitals often cater to foreigners, providing a higher standard of care, but language issues may arise, especially in **public healthcare settings**.

---

34 https://expatfinancial.com/healthcare-information-by-region/
    caribbean-healthcare-system/dominican-republic-healthcare-system/

To access medical services, **private health insurance** is essential for covering medical costs, especially since healthcare can be expensive in tourist areas. International health insurance plans offer comprehensive coverage, including **emergency evacuation** and **repatriation benefits**, making them ideal for visitors staying for longer periods. Local health insurance and **travel insurance** are also options, depending on the visitor's length of stay. Travel insurance typically covers **emergency medical treatment** and **trip-related mishaps**, while international health insurance offers broader coverage, including plans for **long-term stays**. Visitors should be aware that medical services are often provided on a **cash-before-treatment basis**, with costs varying from **US$250** for basic coverage to upwards of **US$1,500** for complex procedures, such as **cataract surgery**.[35]

While **out-of-pocket payments** are available, the standard of care may vary depending on the healthcare provider. Private clinics and hospitals generally provide better services, though they can be expensive. For example, a visit to a **cardiologist** might cost around **US$40**, while **surgical procedures** like cataract surgery could cost approximately **US$1,500 per eye**.[36]

Language barriers are a notable issue, as English is commonly spoken in private healthcare facilities in tourist areas, but less so in public hospitals. Most medical staff in public hospitals may only speak **Spanish**, which can be a challenge for visitors who don't speak the language. Fortunately, many private clinics in tourist areas have staff fluent in English, and there may be translators available to assist with communication, although visitors should remain proactive in ensuring clear communication during medical consultations.

---

35 https://realtordr.com/
    healthcare-in-the-dominican-republic-explained-better-or-worse/

36 https://www.tripadvisor.com/ShowTopic-g147288-i27-k14914691-
    Healthcare_costs_in_the_DR-Dominican_Republic.html

Dominican Hospitals

The Dominican Republic has a well-developed healthcare infrastructure with a combination of **public and private hospitals** spread across the country. The Dominican Republic has approximately **445 hospitals**. These hospitals tend to be **relatively small**, averaging around 25 beds each.[37] In 2022, the country had approximately **2.235 physicians per 1,000 people**.[38] The number of doctors and specialists is concentrated in the **major urban centers**.

Likewise, hospitals are most concentrated in the **Santo Domingo** area, which is the capital and largest city in the country. Other major cities like **Santiago, La Romana**, and **Punta Cana** also have significant healthcare facilities, particularly **private hospitals** that cater to foreign visitors. **Santo Domingo** has the largest and most advanced hospitals, with a wide range of specialized care, while smaller towns or rural areas may have fewer resources. Some of the **best hospitals** in the Dominican Republic include both **public** and **private** institutions. **Public hospitals** such as **Hospital Salvador B. Gautier** and **Hospital General de la Plaza de la Salud** in **Santo Domingo** provide a high standard of care for locals, although they are often crowded and less equipped compared to their private counterparts. For **private healthcare, Hospiten** (with multiple locations including those in **Santo Domingo, Punta Cana**, and **Santiago**) is one of the best options for foreign visitors, offering modern medical facilities and services in English. **Centro de Medicina Avanzada (CMA)** is another top private hospital in **Santo Domingo**, known for its advanced treatment options and specialized care.

The **American Hospital** in the Dominican Republic is **Hospital Metropolitano de Santiago (HOMS)**, located in **Santiago**, which is well-regarded for its American standard of care and often serves expats and international patients. Another American-standard hospital is **Clinica Abreu** in **Santo Domingo**, which is also popular among foreign

---

37   https://globalhealthintelligence.com/tag/
      number-of-hospitals-in-dominican-republic/

38   https://tradingeconomics.com/dominican-republic/physicians-per-1-
      000-people-wb-data.html

residents and tourists. These facilities are equipped with modern medical technology and staff trained in international standards of care, making them particularly suitable for foreign visitors or expatriates in need of high-quality medical attention.

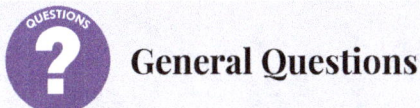 **General Questions**

1. *What should you do if you feel unwell/sick in the Dominican Republic?* If you feel unwell in the Dominican Republic, start by visiting a pharmacy for minor ailments, as they are widely available and often provide over-the-counter medications. For more severe or persistent symptoms, seek medical attention at a private clinic or hospital like Hospiten or Centro de Medicina Avanzada, where care is more accessible for foreigners. If you have travel insurance, contact your provider for guidance and coverage details. In case of an emergency, call **911** for an ambulance. Be prepared to pay upfront for services, as many private facilities require cash or card payment.

2. *Are there any specialized medical facilities in the Dominican Republic for travelers who need urgent care or evacuation services?* **Yes.** There are specialized medical facilities in the Dominican Republic for travelers needing urgent care or evacuation services. Private hospitals like Hospiten and Centro de Medicina Avanzada in areas such as Santo Domingo, Punta Cana, and Santiago offer emergency medical services and are equipped for urgent conditions and specialized treatments. For medical evacuation, private hospitals and travel insurance providers can arrange air ambulance services for rapid evacuation, with coverage often included in emergency assistance plans. It's important to confirm evacuation coverage with your insurance before traveling.

Here are the most important contact numbers, essential for accessing urgent medical, police, or fire services across the country. In tourist areas, many services are available in **English** to assist foreign visitors.

911 – Emergency services (ambulance, fire, police)

809-200-7373 – National Ambulance Service (for non-911 emergencies)

132 – Fire Department

110 – Police

165 – Tourist Police (for assistance to foreign visitors)

Insurance Guidance

Foreign insurance plans are **generally accepted** in **private healthcare facilities** in the Dominican Republic, especially in larger cities like Santo Domingo, Punta Cana, and Santiago. Many hospitals and clinics are familiar with international health insurance providers and can directly bill them for medical services. However, it's important to **confirm** with the medical facility whether your specific plan is accepted and ensure that your policy covers medical care and emergency evacuation.

The **average costs** for medical services in the Dominican Republic can vary depending on the type of care needed. A visit to the **emergency room** typically costs between **US$50-200** for basic services, while more specialized care (like surgeries or tests) can cost significantly more. A **general doctor's visit** usually costs between **US$30-75**, and more specialized consultations, like with a **cardiologist** or **orthopedist**, can range from **US$60-150**.

Most medical facilities in the Dominican Republic require **payment upfront** before services are provided, especially for foreign patients. You can pay by **credit card** or **cash** (USD or Dominican pesos). If you are using **insurance**, you may be required to **pay out-of-pocket** first and submit a claim later for reimbursement, depending on the hospital and your insurance policy. Always check with your insurance provider for details on direct billing or reimbursement processes before seeking treatment.

DRIVING IN THE DOMINICAN REPUBLIC

IN THIS CHAPTER

- Overview
- Main Traffic Rules & Road Safety Tips
- General Questions
- Law of the Land Hypothetical

DRIVING IN THE DOMINICAN REPUBLIC

Overview

Driving in the Dominican Republic offers a unique and sometimes challenging experience, especially for those unfamiliar with the local driving culture. The overall driving environment can feel somewhat **chaotic**, especially in urban areas like Santo Domingo. Drivers often display aggressive behaviors, such as frequent lane changes without signaling, tailgating, and disregarding speed limits. While road conditions in major cities and on some highways are improving, rural roads can be poorly maintained, with potholes, uneven surfaces, and a lack of proper signage. Road lighting is also often inadequate outside urban centers, making nighttime driving particularly difficult.

Foreign drivers are allowed to use their **home country's driver's license** for up to **90 days**. However, it's recommended to carry an **international drivers permit** (**IDP**), as it provides a translation of your home license. If you're renting a vehicle, the rental agency will typically handle all necessary registration and insurance paperwork. For those bringing their own cars into the country, it's important to ensure that your vehicle is properly registered and insured, as you may be asked to provide documentation in the event of an accident. Having **insurance is strongly recommended**, whether you're renting or driving your own car, as it is a legal requirement in case of an accident.

When driving, you'll notice some **unique customs** and driving signals. **Honking** your horn is a common way for drivers to communicate with each other. It might signal anything from announcing a passing maneuver to expressing frustration or simply alerting other drivers of your presence. **Speed bumps**, or "*topes*," are also a prominent feature of the Dominican road system, especially in rural areas, and they can be very high and sometimes unmarked, so caution is needed. **Roundabouts** are frequently used, but Dominican drivers don't always follow the expected right-of-way rules, which can make these areas unpredictable. **Motorcycles**, which are a common mode of transport, often weave through traffic and may appear suddenly. Additionally, **pedestrians and animals**—especially livestock—frequently cross roads, particularly outside urban areas, so drivers should stay alert for these unexpected obstacles.

Toll roads are common in the Dominican Republic, particularly highways like **the Autopista Duarte** that connects Santo Domingo to Santiago. These toll roads are a faster and more efficient way to travel long distances but come with a fee. Payment is generally made in Dominican pesos at toll booths, but credit cards are accepted at some locations. Increasingly, toll booths are equipped with electronic payment systems, allowing for quicker and more convenient toll payments, which are ideal for those traveling frequently or looking to avoid long lines. The cost of tolls isn't typically high, with most tolls ranging from **RD$50-200** (about US$1-4), though the total can add up if you're traveling over long distances or through multiple toll booths.

Despite the challenges, driving in the Dominican Republic can be a rewarding way to explore the country. If you stay alert, drive defensively, and take extra caution in areas with poor infrastructure or heavy traffic, you can enjoy a memorable experience. Always be mindful of local customs and the road conditions, and if possible, avoid driving at night in rural or unfamiliar areas.

 # Main Traffic Rules & Road Safety Tips

- **Driving Side:** Right side of the road.

- **Speed Limits:**

  - **Highways and toll roads:** 100 km/h (62 mph).

  - **Urban areas:** 60 km/h (37 mph), with residential and school zones often having lower limits, such as 40 km/h (25 mph).

- **Traffic Signals:**

  - Red means stop, green means go, yellow signals caution or prepare to stop.

  - Drivers may not always strictly adhere to signals, and pedestrian crossings may not be respected. Roundabout right-of-way rules are often ignored.

- **Seat Belts:**

  - Mandatory for all passengers.

  - Failure to wear a seatbelt can result in a fine, especially in urban areas.

- **Alcohol:**

  - **Blood alcohol limit: 0.05 percent for private drivers, 0.00 percent for commercial drivers.**

  - Driving under the influence is a serious offense, with penalties including fines, license suspension, or jail time. Sobriety checkpoints are common.

- **Mobile Devices:**

  - Using a mobile phone while driving is illegal unless hands-free.

  - Fines apply for texting or holding a phone while driving. Enforcement is stricter in urban areas.

- **Toll Roads:**

  - Several toll roads, particularly between major cities.

  - Payments can be made in Dominican pesos or by credit card. Electronic toll systems are also used, with tolls typically ranging from RD$50-200 (US$1-4).

- **If Stopped by Police:**

  - Remain calm and respectful.

  - Show your driver's license, vehicle registration, and insurance. Foreign drivers may need an international driver's permit (IDP). Bribery may be requested in some cases, but it's best to ask for a receipt for fines.

- **Road Safety Tips:**

  - Stay alert for motorcyclists, cyclists, pedestrians, animals, and other drivers who may not follow traffic rules.

  - Avoid night driving, especially outside major cities.

  - Drive cautiously in rural areas with poorly maintained roads.

  - Know local road signs, many of which are in Spanish or have local variations.

  - Plan your route, especially for long distances or unfamiliar areas.

  - Ensure your vehicle is adequately insured, whether renting or driving your own car.

General Questions

1. ***Can I use my driver's license from my home country to drive in the Dominican Republic?*** Yes. You can use your driver's license from your home country to drive in the Dominican Republic for up to **90 days**. However, it's recommended to also carry an **International Driver's Permit** (**IDP**), especially if your license is not in Spanish, as it provides a translation of your home license. The IDP is not mandatory, but it can make things easier if you need to deal with authorities or rental agencies.

2. ***What is the age requirement for renting a car in the Dominican Republic?*** The **minimum age** for renting a car in the Dominican Republic is typically **21 years old**, though some rental companies may require you to be at least **25 years old** to rent certain types of vehicles or avoid additional young driver surcharges. If you're under 25, you may be subject to an **additional fee** for being a "young driver." Also, you will generally need to have held a valid driver's license for at least **two years** to rent a car.

Law of the Land Hypothetical

HYPOTHETICAL: *John, a 35-year-old tourist from the United States, is visiting the Dominican Republic for business. He plans to drive from Santo Domingo to Punta Cana. At the rental agency, John presents his U.S. driver's license and is asked if he has an International Driver's Permit (IDP). John replies that he doesn't have one, believing his U.S. license is enough. The agent explains that while his license is valid, an IDP is highly recommended for non-Spanish-speaking drivers. Is John required to have an International Driver's Permit (IDP) to drive in the Dominican Republic with his U.S. driver's license?*

ANSWER: *No. John is **not required** to have an IDP to drive in the Dominican Republic for **up to 90 days**. His U.S. driver's license is valid for driving in the country. However, an IDP is recommended, especially for non-Spanish-speaking drivers, as it translates the license and can help if there are any issues with local authorities. While John can drive without it, having an IDP would make interactions with authorities easier and avoid complications.*

NUDE BEACHES & CLOTHING-OPTIONAL RESORTS

IN THIS CHAPTER

- Overview
- Legality and Safety
- General Questions
- Law of the Land Hypothetical

NUDE BEACHES & CLOTHING-OPTIONAL RESORTS

Overview

Nudism is **not generally accepted** in the Dominican Republic due to the country's more conservative cultural and social attitudes toward public decency and attire. **Public nudity** is **prohibited**, and local norms emphasize modesty, particularly in public spaces such as city streets, beaches, and towns. Dominicans typically view modest dress as important, and wearing swimwear outside of beach areas is often frowned upon.

However, there are some exceptions where nudism is allowed in controlled, private environments. Certain **secluded beaches** or **private resorts** cater specifically to those seeking a nudist-friendly experience. For example, **Bahía de las Águilas**, located in the southwest of the country, is one of the more remote and less-developed beaches where nudism is tolerated. Although it isn't officially promoted as a nudist beach, the area's isolation and natural beauty make it a popular spot for those seeking privacy and the freedom to engage in clothing-optional activities.

Despite the general prohibition on public nudity, there are specific venues where naturists can enjoy a clothing-optional environment. **Caliente Caribe** is an all-inclusive, clothing-optional resort located near Cabrera on the northeastern coast. Another venue is **Temptation Grand Miches Resort**, situated about an hour from the Punta Cana airport, which offers a clothing-optional environment for couples.[39] While these are two of very few dedicated nudist resorts in the country, other resorts may allow nudity in specific areas, but it's typically confined to private pools or certain sections of the property.

Legality and Safety[40]

In the Dominican Republic, **nudism is not officially regulated** by the government, as it is generally not a part of the mainstream culture. Public nudity is **illegal**, and the country adheres to traditional values surrounding decency and modesty, particularly in public spaces. Therefore, any form of nudity outside of designated areas is not permitted and could lead to legal consequences, including fines or potential arrest for indecent exposure.

However, **nudism is allowed and regulated in specific private spaces**, such as resorts and certain secluded beaches, where the practice is tolerated under controlled conditions. These places are typically all-inclusive or exclusive resorts that market themselves as **clothing-optional** or **nude-friendly**, and they have their own set of guidelines to ensure that guests respect the privacy and comfort of others. These guidelines help prevent any cultural conflicts or misunderstandings with local residents.

When it comes to **nudist etiquette**, visitors should be mindful of the following expectations:

- **Respect the boundaries of designated areas:** Nudism is only acceptable in specific private areas. Guests should never be nude in public spaces or in places where others may not expect it, such as local beaches, bars, or restaurants.

- **Ask for permission:** In a private resort or hotel that permits nudism, always check the rules regarding the appropriate areas and the proper behavior in public spaces. Not all resorts will allow nudity

---

39 https://sandee.com/blog/nudism-laws-in-dominican-republic

40 https://www.beachatlas.com/nudism-laws-dominican-republic

everywhere, so it's important to follow the establishment's specific guidelines.

- **Be discreet in interactions:** While nudity might be allowed in private settings, engaging in sexual or inappropriate behavior in public is not tolerated. Respect for fellow guests is crucial, and maintaining appropriate decorum ensures a pleasant and safe environment for everyone.

- **Respect local culture:** Outside of designated nudist spaces, the general culture of the Dominican Republic is modest. Visitors should avoid being nude in public, on regular beaches, or in public areas, as this would be disrespectful and illegal.

 ## General Questions

1. *Can foreign tourists practice nudism in the Dominican Republic without issues?* **Yes**. Foreign tourists can practice nudism in the Dominican Republic, but it is important to do so in the right contexts. While the country is not known for a widespread nudist culture, tourists can enjoy clothing-optional resorts and certain private beaches where nudism is permitted. These areas are specifically designed to cater to those seeking a nudist experience, and the rules around nudity are clearly defined within these spaces. However, outside of these areas, nudism is considered illegal and socially inappropriate, and tourists should avoid engaging in nudism in public settings, as it could lead to legal consequences or cultural misunderstandings. To ensure a safe and enjoyable experience, tourists should respect the local customs and only practice nudism in designated areas.

2. ***What are the safety considerations for practicing nudism in the Dominican Republic?*** When practicing nudism in the Dominican Republic, safety largely depends on the environment and the location. Private resorts or clothing-optional beaches that cater to nudists are generally safe spaces, as they are designed to provide privacy and a comfortable environment. In these places, guests can expect to be surrounded by others who share similar interests, which minimizes the risk of unwanted attention or harassment. However, outside these controlled spaces, practicing nudism in public or semi-public areas can be risky, both legally and in terms of personal safety. In such areas, there is a higher likelihood of encountering unwanted attention from locals or other tourists, as well as potential legal issues if caught in violation of local laws regarding public decency. Additionally, the lack of privacy in non-designated areas can make individuals vulnerable to opportunistic theft or harassment.

 **Law of the Land Hypothetical**

HYPOTHETICAL: *Anna, a 28-year-old tourist from the U.S., is staying at a clothing-optional resort in Bavaro and visits the secluded Playa Macao beach. She decides to go topless while walking along the beach. A local fisherman sees her and, feeling uncomfortable, tells her to cover up. Can the fisherman legally report Anna for being topless, and is she protected by Dominican law?*

ANSWER: *Yes. The fisherman can report Anna for public nudity, which is illegal in the Dominican Republic. While public nudity is not allowed, even in secluded areas, Anna is not protected under the law for being topless on a public beach. The Dominican Penal Code prohibits indecent exposure in public spaces, and she could face fines or other penalties. To avoid legal trouble, Anna should comply with the fisherman's request and cover up. Although she might not face serious legal consequences, it's safer to follow local customs and avoid nudity outside of designated nudist areas or private resorts.*

CHAPTER 20
UNUSUAL LAWS

IN THIS CHAPTER

- Overview
- Unusual Dominican Laws and Associated Penalties
- General Questions
- Law of the Land Hypothetical

UNUSUAL LAWS

Overview

Unusual laws can be fascinating glimpses into a culture's values and history. While most people are aware of common legal restrictions, it's often the strange and quirky laws that capture our attention. These regulations can range from the amusing to the absurd, reflecting the unique circumstances and traditions of a place. Whether they arise from historical events, societal norms, or simply peculiar local customs, unusual laws can provide insight into the quirks of human behavior and governance.

 **Unusual Dominican Laws and Associated Penalties**

The Dominican Republic has some unique and quirky laws that might seem unusual to visitors, and it's important for tourists to be aware of them to avoid any legal issues during their stay. Here are a few examples:

Prohibition of Camouflage Clothing

It's illegal to wear camouflage clothing in the Dominican Republic. This law is in place to prevent confusion with military personnel and maintain public order. Although it's not strictly enforced everywhere, wearing camouflage can attract unwanted attention from authorities.

Penalty: Violators may be asked to change their clothing and could face fines or other minor consequences.

Prohibition on Selling Alcohol During Certain Hours

In the Dominican Republic, there are specific laws regulating when alcohol can be sold. In some regions, alcohol sales are prohibited on Sundays, and the hours of sale may vary. This is more common in more conservative areas or around religious holidays.

Penalty: Stores or individuals caught selling alcohol outside of the designated hours can be fined or temporarily shut down.

Departure Tax

Travelers leaving the Dominican Republic are required to pay a **US$20 departure tax**. This is often included in the cost of airline tickets, but if not, it must be paid at the airport before departure.

Penalty: Failure to pay the departure tax could result in being denied boarding until the fee is settled.

Littering

Littering in public spaces, especially in tourist areas like beaches or streets, is strictly prohibited. While this might seem like a common-sense law, it is rigorously enforced in some areas to maintain cleanliness and tourism appeal.

Penalty: Those caught littering can face fines or be required to clean the area where the litter was disposed of. Severe violations could result in more significant legal actions.

General Questions

1. ***What are the legal consequences for wearing camouflage clothing in the Dominican Republic, and why is this law in place?***
   Wearing camouflage clothing in the Dominican Republic is illegal
   for civilians due to the law aimed at preventing confusion with
   military personnel. The government enforces this to maintain
   public order and avoid situations where individuals could be
   mistaken for members of the armed forces. While the law is not
   always strictly enforced, it is advisable for both locals and tourists
   to avoid wearing camouflage clothing. If caught, violators may
   face fines or confiscation of the clothing.

2. ***What are the rules and penalties for overcrowding in "conchos" (shared taxis) in the Dominican Republic?*** In the
   Dominican Republic, "conchos" (shared taxis) are regulated to
   carry a specific number of passengers based on the vehicle's seating capacity. Overcrowding occurs when this limit is exceeded,
   such as fitting more passengers than the vehicle can safely accommodate. Penalties for overcrowding include fines for the driver
   and potential impoundment of the vehicle. While enforcement
   is stricter in larger cities like Santo Domingo, it may be more
   lenient in rural areas. Overcrowding poses safety risks, making
   rides uncomfortable and increasing the likelihood of injury in
   case of an accident due to a lack of proper seating. Both drivers
   and passengers should follow these limits to ensure safety and
   avoid legal issues.

Law of the Land Hypothetical

HYPOTHETICAL: *James, a tourist visiting the Dominican Republic, is
enjoying a relaxing day at the beach. While taking a walk along the
shoreline, he notices a vendor selling seashell necklaces. However, when*

he hands over his money, the vendor is stopped by a local official, who informs James that it's illegal to purchase certain types of seashells. Why is it illegal to buy seashells or related souvenirs in the Dominican Republic, and what are the potential consequences for violating this law?

ANSWER: *In the Dominican Republic, buying seashells, particularly those from protected species, is prohibited by law to protect the country's marine environment and biodiversity. The government has implemented regulations to prevent the trade in endangered marine life and protect fragile ecosystems. If James were caught purchasing a protected seashell, he could face fines, and the item could be confiscated. Tourists should be mindful of local environmental laws and avoid purchasing souvenirs made from endangered species to avoid legal trouble and help preserve the country's wildlife.*

TRAVELING SAFELY

- Ladies Traveling Solo
- Traveling as a Family
- Advice for All Travelers
- Do's and Don'ts While in the Dominican Republic

TRAVELING SAFELY

Ladies Traveling Solo[41]

The Dominican Republic is generally considered **safe for travelers**, but, like any destination, it's important to stay aware of your surroundings. It's a popular destination, particularly for those seeking beaches and vibrant culture, and many women travel there solo each year. The country has a reputation for friendly locals and an extensive tourism infrastructure, especially in areas like Punta Cana, Puerto Plata, and Santo Domingo. However, the country also faces challenges with crime, including **petty theft** and **occasional violent crime**, particularly outside tourist zones. Solo female travelers may experience both positive and negative situations, and it's **important to exercise caution**.

In terms of safety for women traveling alone, many report feeling comfortable in major tourist areas where security is typically visible. However, like in any foreign country, certain risks exist. Women may encounter **unsolicited attention**, such as street harassment, particularly in crowded areas or where tourists are concentrated. While some women have had great experiences in the Dominican Republic, others note that there are moments when it's important to be more cautious. Speaking the local language, Spanish, even at a basic level, can be helpful in avoiding misunderstandings and navigating situations more easily.

---

41 https://www.globalguardian.com/global-digest/
    is-dominican-republic-safe

There are areas that solo travelers, especially women, should be more cautious about. In Santo Domingo, for example, certain neighborhoods like **La Ciénaga** and **Villa Mella** are known to have higher crime rates and are generally less safe after dark. Similarly, parts of **Puerto Plata** and areas around **Boca Chica** can pose risks, particularly in remote or less-policed zones. While the popular beach areas may seem inviting, **isolated beaches** and **less-traveled streets** should be avoided after dark.

Safety precautions are essential to ensure a positive experience. It's recommended to stick to well-known, tourist-friendly areas, particularly if you're unfamiliar with the country. Many solo travelers prefer staying in **all-inclusive resorts** or **reputable hotels**, where security is typically more robust. Modest clothing can help you blend in better in local, non-tourist areas, reducing the likelihood of unwanted attention. If you're in a busy area, **be mindful of pickpockets** and keep your belongings secure. Using a crossbody bag with zippers is a simple but effective measure. When it comes to transportation, it's best to rely on **taxis arranged by your hotel** or use trusted **rideshare services** like Uber, especially after dark. Public transportation, while cheap, can sometimes be uncomfortable and risky in certain areas.

Drinking alcohol responsibly is another important precaution. Never accept drinks from strangers and **avoid excessive drinking** in unfamiliar settings. If you do plan on drinking, try to stay in the company of others. It's also wise to avoid walking alone after dark, especially in less populated or poorly lit areas. If you must go out at night, opt for a trusted form of transportation or take a group with you. Stay connected with friends or family back home, sharing your itinerary and checking in regularly. Trusting your instincts is perhaps the most important safety measure. If something feels off, it's better to remove yourself from the situation rather than risk it.

Having a **basic knowledge of Spanish** can go a long way in helping you feel more confident and able to handle situations. Learning how to ask for help or directions can be a lifesaver, especially if you find yourself in a pinch. Travel insurance is highly recommended, covering both medical emergencies and theft or cancellations. Lastly, ensure you have any **necessary vaccinations** before traveling to the Dominican Republic, and consider carrying a small first aid kit in case of minor health issues.

While there are risks, many solo female travelers visit the Dominican Republic without issue, and by staying aware and prepared, you can enjoy the country safely. It's important to balance exploration with caution, allowing you to experience the beauty of the Dominican Republic while minimizing potential risks.

Traveling as a Family

Traveling to the Dominican Republic with children can be a fantastic experience, but it's important to take necessary **safety** and **health precautions** to ensure a smooth and enjoyable trip. When it comes to safety, always supervise your children, especially around water. The ocean currents can be strong, and pool areas should be monitored at all times. It's essential to be cautious of traffic in urban areas, as road conditions and driving habits may differ from what you're used to. Always use car seats for younger children and avoid letting kids wander in busy areas.

In terms of health, make sure your children are up to date on vaccinations before traveling.[42] It's advisable to get additional vaccines like **Hepatitis A** and **Typhoid**. Water in the Dominican Republic may not always be safe to drink, so always opt for **bottled water** and avoid consuming ice or tap water. When it comes to food, stick to **well-cooked meals** and avoid raw or undercooked items. Insects, particularly **mosquitoes**, can carry diseases such as Zika and Dengue, so it's important to apply insect repellent and dress children in long sleeves and pants, especially during dusk and dawn.

The sun in the Dominican Republic can be very intense, so make sure to apply sunscreen frequently and encourage your children to take breaks in the shade. A basic first aid kit is a must, including essentials like band-aids, pain relievers, and any prescription medications your children may need. Consider buying **travel insurance** that covers medical emergencies, as healthcare in some areas may not meet the same standards you're used to.

---

42 https://www.passporthealthusa.com/destination-advice/
    dominican-republic/

To make the trip enjoyable, plan family-friendly activities, such as beach trips, exploring natural pools, or visiting adventure parks. Prepare for the tropical climate by packing light, breathable clothing and always carrying a water bottle. If you're traveling from a different time zone, adjust your child's sleep schedule in advance to minimize jet lag. By taking these precautions, you'll ensure a safer, more comfortable experience for your family in the Dominican Republic.

Advice for All Travelers

When traveling to the Dominican Republic, it's important to stay mindful of a few things to ensure a safe and enjoyable trip. Scams and tourist traps are common, so be cautious of unsolicited services and always negotiate prices upfront, especially in markets or for transport. Petty theft, like pickpocketing, can occur in crowded areas, so keep an eye on your belongings, avoid carrying large amounts of cash, and use hotel safes for valuables.

Traffic can be chaotic, particularly in cities like Santo Domingo, so if you plan to drive, be extra careful. If unfamiliar with local roads, consider hiring a driver. Also, always cross streets cautiously and use designated crosswalks. Tap water isn't safe to drink, so stick to bottled water, even when brushing your teeth, and avoid consuming ice.

Mosquitoes are prevalent and can carry diseases like Zika and Dengue, so use insect repellent, especially during dawn and dusk. Protect yourself from the sun with sunscreen, hats, and sunglasses, and stay hydrated to avoid heat exhaustion. Drug laws are strict, and even small amounts of illegal substances can lead to serious consequences, so avoid any involvement with drugs.

While the beaches are stunning, be cautious of strong currents and waves. Always check with locals or lifeguards before swimming. When using ATMs, choose machines located inside secure areas to avoid card skimming. Lastly, be respectful of local customs and traditions. Dress modestly when visiting religious sites and ask permission before taking photos of people, especially in rural areas.

Do's and Don'ts While in the Dominican Republic

When visiting the Dominican Republic, understanding and respecting local customs can greatly enhance your experience. The country places a strong emphasis on family, hospitality, and social connections, so being mindful of cultural norms is key. Whether it's how you greet someone or how you interact in social situations, small gestures can go a long way in showing respect for Dominican traditions. Here are some Do's and Don'ts while in the Dominican Republic:

- **Do greet warmly with a kiss on the cheek.** In the Dominican Republic, it's customary to greet people with a kiss on the right cheek, even if you've just met. This is a sign of warmth and friendliness, especially in informal settings.

- **Don't criticize local politics or leaders.** Discussions about politics, especially the government or political figures, can be sensitive. Avoid offering negative opinions about Dominican politics or leaders to prevent causing discomfort.

- **Do embrace the rhythm of bachata and merengue.** Dance is deeply embedded in Dominican culture, with bachata and merengue being particularly popular. If you're invited to dance, even if you're not a dancer, joining in is a great way to connect with the locals.

- **Don't argue or raise your voice in public.** Dominicans value harmony, and public disputes are discouraged. Speaking loudly or aggressively can be seen as disrespectful. Keep conversations calm and friendly, especially in social settings.

- **Do dress casually but with respect.** While the country is warm and casual attire is common, make sure to dress modestly when visiting religious sites or attending formal gatherings. Avoid overly revealing clothing to show respect for local customs.

- **Don't arrive exactly on time for social events.** In the Dominican Republic, arriving 15 to 30 minutes late for a party or family gathering is perfectly normal. Being too punctual may even seem rushed or impolite.

TOURIST TAXATION

IN THIS CHAPTER

- Overview
- Tourist Taxes in the Dominican Republic
- Law of the Land Hypothetical

TOURIST TAXATION

Overview[43]

Tourism plays a significant role in the Dominican Republic's economy, contributing substantially to employment, foreign exchange earnings, and overall GDP. As **one of the most visited destinations in the Caribbean**, tourism supports a wide range of industries, including hospitality, transportation, retail, and agriculture. The sector is crucial to the nation's economic framework, providing jobs for thousands of locals and driving growth in both urban and rural areas.

Tourism has grown into a crucial component of the Dominican Republic's economy, accounting for 15 percent to 16 percent of the country's GDP, including indirect impacts. The service sector, which includes tourism, generated 61 percent of the GDP and over 70 percent of the country's employment in 2019. In 2021, the tourism sector contributed about 38 percent to the country's economic recovery, demonstrating its resilience and importance.[44]

Tourists are required to pay taxes in the Dominican Republic to help fund the various public services and infrastructure that make the country an attractive destination. These taxes are essential for maintaining

---

43 https://everythingpuntacana.com/tourist-card-punta-cana/)

44 https://www.unwto.org/investment/
tourism-doing-business-investing-in-dominican-republic

and improving the **country's tourism-related services**, such as airports, roads, and healthcare systems, which benefit both visitors and locals. Tourist taxes can be levied in several ways, including **departure taxes**, **hotel taxes**, and **specific fees for tours or activities**. These taxes are seen as a way to ensure that the tourism industry contributes to the public good, while also helping to sustain the growth of the sector itself.

Tourist taxes help support **public services** and **infrastructure** by generating revenue that can be reinvested into essential services, like education, healthcare, public safety, and environmental conservation. Additionally, the revenue collected from tourists allows the government to maintain and upgrade vital infrastructure, such as the country's roads, airports, and public transport systems, which in turn enhances the overall tourist experience and promotes sustainable growth. By contributing through these taxes, tourists indirectly help improve the quality of life for residents and ensure that the Dominican Republic remains a competitive and attractive destination for future travelers.

Tourist Taxes in the Dominican Republic

The Dominican Republic has several types of tourist taxes that are levied on both visitors and businesses operating in the tourism sector, primarily aimed at generating revenue for the government and supporting the country's tourism infrastructure. The main types of tourist taxes in the Dominican Republic include:

- **Airport Departure Tax:** This tax is collected when tourists depart from the Dominican Republic via international flight, usually included in the price of the plane ticket. If it's not, the tax can be paid at the airport either in cash (in US dollars or Dominican Pesos) or by credit card before boarding the flight. The standard departure tax is **US$20** per person.

- **Tourism Entry Tax (Tourist Card):** This is a tax that tourists are required to pay when entering the country. It can be purchased at the airport upon arrival or online in advance. It is typically included in the airline ticket price for many international flights, so passengers might not need to buy it separately. The tourist card costs **$US10** (as of the last update).

- **Tourist Services Tax (Excursions, Transport, etc.):** Certain services related to tourism, such as excursions, transportation, and tours, may be subject to a **10 percent** tax. It is typically included in the total price of the service, and tourists may not need to make a separate payment.

- **Value Added Tax (VAT) on Tourism Services:** The general VAT in the Dominican Republic is **18 percent**. However, the government has provisions for a reduced rate or exemption on specific tourism-related services like hotel accommodations, transportation, and some other tourism services. This is added directly to the price of the service, and businesses in the tourism sector are responsible for remitting it to the government.

 **Important Points to Note**

- Taxes like the departure tax or tourist card tax are only applicable to international travel.

- Some taxes, like the tourist card, can be paid online in advance, which may save time at the airport.

 **Law of the Land Hypothetical**

HYPOTHETICAL: *Maria, a tourist from Spain, arrives at the airport in the Dominican Republic. She is asked to pay the US$10 Tourist Card fee. Maria thinks the fee is included in her airline ticket, but the immigration officer explains that she must pay it separately unless her*

airline included it. Is it legal for Maria to be asked to pay the US$10 Tourist Card fee, and should it have been included in her airline ticket?

ANSWER: *Yes.* *It is legal for Maria to be required to pay the US$10 Tourist Card fee upon arrival. The fee is mandatory for most international tourists entering the Dominican Republic, and it is not automatically included in every airline ticket. While some airlines may include the fee in the ticket price, it is not a requirement for all airlines. Maria should have confirmed with her airline whether the fee was included in her ticket before traveling. The immigration officer's request for payment was entirely in accordance with Dominican law.*

CHAPTER 23
LONG-TERM STAYS

IN THIS CHAPTER

- Overview
- Long-Term Visas
- General Questions
- Law of the Land Hypothetical
- Law of the Land True Story
- Takeaways

LONG-TERM STAYS

Overview

Many people choose to live in the Dominican Republic long-term for its appealing combination of **warm weather, affordable living costs**, and the ease of accessing its **beautiful beaches, mountains**, and **natural parks**. For retirees, the **relatively low cost of healthcare** and the ability to live comfortably on a pension or savings is a significant draw. Additionally, the country's **growing expat community** offers a sense of familiarity, making it easier for newcomers to integrate. For others, the country's proximity to the U.S. makes it a **great base for travel** while maintaining easy access to family and friends in North America.

Employment opportunities are also available, especially for those in tourism, hospitality, or teaching English, although the job market might not be as robust as in other countries, particularly for foreigners. Digital nomads are increasingly attracted to the Dominican Republic due to its affordable living and fast internet infrastructure, especially in cities like Santo Domingo or Puerto Plata.

The Dominican Republic has a variety of regions that cater to different lifestyles. **Santo Domingo**, the capital, is the largest city and offers modern amenities, healthcare, and a bustling job market, making it ideal for those who enjoy urban life. It's a vibrant cultural hub, with historical sites, shopping, dining, and entertainment options. For those seeking a more relaxed pace of life, coastal towns like **Punta Cana**, **Cabarete**, and

Las Terrenas are popular choices. These areas offer stunning beaches, an easygoing lifestyle, and a growing expat community. Punta Cana, in particular, has a well-developed infrastructure for both tourists and long-term residents, including international schools, modern shopping centers, and excellent healthcare facilities.

If you're drawn to the cooler mountain air, places like **Jarabacoa** and **Constanza**, located in the Central Highlands, offer picturesque landscapes, hiking, and a quieter lifestyle. These regions are becoming increasingly popular with retirees and expats seeking a slower pace of life surrounded by nature.

Living Costs in the Dominican Republic

The Dominican Republic offers a **significantly lower cost of living** compared to countries like the U.S., Canada, and much of Europe. Rent, groceries, and utilities are typically much more affordable, making it an attractive option for those looking to stretch their budget further. For example, **rent** for a one-bedroom apartment in Santo Domingo can be found for as low as **US$400-600 per month**, and utilities are generally affordable, though they can fluctuate based on location and lifestyle.

Dining out is also budget-friendly, with a wide range of options from street food to upscale restaurants. Monthly grocery expenses are lower than in the U.S., though imported goods can sometimes be more expensive. Public transportation is affordable, though not as comprehensive as in larger cities around the world, so many expats prefer to drive.

Overall, the Dominican Republic provides a good balance between affordable living and access to modern amenities. In comparison with countries in Western Europe, the U.S., or even many parts of Latin America, living costs here are quite manageable.

Housing Options for Long-Term Stays

Housing options in the Dominican Republic are diverse, ranging from **affordable apartments** in the city to **luxurious villas** in coastal areas. Rent is generally more affordable than in many Western countries, and there are many **expat-friendly neighborhoods**, especially in the capital, Santo Domingo, and beach towns like Punta Cana, Cabarete, and Sosúa. Whether you're looking for a modern apartment or a more traditional Caribbean-style home, the market offers something for almost every budget.

In urban areas, rental prices can range widely depending on the location and amenities. For example, a one-bedroom apartment in the heart of Santo Domingo might cost between US$400-700 per month, while similar properties in smaller towns or rural areas could be much cheaper. Many expats prefer to rent before committing to purchasing property, although buying real estate in the Dominican Republic is also an option, and the process is relatively straightforward for foreigners, with some restrictions on beachfront property.

Healthcare Options Available for Long-Term Residents

The Dominican Republic offers both public and private healthcare systems, with a noticeable difference in quality and accessibility between the two. The **public healthcare system** can be under-resourced and is **not always the best option for expats**, especially for more specialized care. However, **private healthcare** is widely available and of a **high standard**, with many doctors and medical professionals trained abroad, particularly in cities like Santo Domingo and Santiago.

Many long-term residents opt for private health insurance, which is **affordable** compared to North American or European premiums. There are several international insurance providers operating in the Dominican Republic, as well as local options. Private healthcare facilities in major cities offer a wide range of services, from general care to advanced medical treatments, often at a fraction of the cost of what you would pay in countries like the U.S.

Transportation Options

Transportation in the Dominican Republic varies depending on location. In cities like Santo Domingo, public transportation options include **buses** and the **metro system**, though coverage and frequency can sometimes be inconsistent. Many expats prefer to rely on **private transportation**, either by owning a **car** or using **taxis** and **ride-sharing services** like Uber. **Car rentals** are also popular for short-term stays, but owning a car is often seen as more convenient for long-term residents, particularly outside of urban centers.

In tourist-heavy areas like Punta Cana, public transport options are limited, so owning a car or using ride-sharing apps is common. Some regions, especially rural areas, may have more limited public transport, and driving becomes necessary. Road conditions vary, with urban areas typically having well-maintained roads, while rural regions may have more rugged or poorly maintained infrastructure.

Language Considerations

Spanish is the official language of the Dominican Republic, and while **English** is commonly spoken in tourist areas and among expats, especially in major cities like Santo Domingo or Punta Cana, it's helpful for long-term residents to learn Spanish. Many Dominicans speak some English, particularly in the hospitality industry, but for deeper integration—whether in work, socializing, or dealing with bureaucracy—learning Spanish will significantly enhance your experience and ease of living.

Language schools and private tutors are available, especially in larger cities. For those who don't speak Spanish fluently, getting by is still possible, but embracing the local language will improve your quality of life and help you feel more at home in the community.

Long-Term Visas[45]

For those considering a long-term stay in the Dominican Republic, there are **several visa options available**, each catering to different types of residents, whether you're planning to retire, work, or invest. Understanding these visa options is crucial for a smooth and legal long-term stay in the country.

---

45 https://visaindex.com/visa/dominican-republic-visa/

The most common visa options for long-term stays in the Dominican Republic are:

Residence Visa (Temporary and Permanent)

The Dominican Republic offers a residence visa that allows foreigners to live in the country long-term. This visa is divided into two main categories: temporary residence and permanent residence. A **temporary residence visa** is generally valid for one year and can be renewed. After two years of holding temporary residence, you can apply for **permanent residence**, which is valid for an indefinite period and provides more stability.

To qualify for temporary residence, applicants must meet **various requirements**, such as having a clean criminal record, providing proof of income (typically showing you can financially support yourself), and undergoing a health examination. For permanent residence, the process is similar but requires additional proof of integration into the country.

Pensioner or Retiree Visa

For retirees or those living off a pension, the Dominican Republic offers a special visa designed for individuals receiving a pension or regular income from abroad. To qualify for a **pensionado visa**, applicants must demonstrate a monthly income of at least **US$1,500** from a pension or retirement fund, along with a one-time application fee and other supporting documents. This visa grants a **temporary residency status**, which can be extended and, eventually, converted into permanent residency. The **pensionado visa** also offers some attractive benefits, such as discounts on utilities, transportation, and healthcare services, making it particularly appealing for retirees looking for a lower cost of living.

Investor Visa

For those interested in starting a business or investing in the Dominican Republic, the **investor visa** is an attractive option. This visa is available for individuals who invest a certain amount of capital into the country, typically in real estate, a business, or a project that generates employment. The minimum required investment varies but is generally around **US$200,000**. The initial investor visa is issued with a validity of just one year. Upon first renewal, however, subsequent visas are valid for four years and can be renewed indefinitely as long as the investment is maintained.

Student Visa

Students who plan to study in the Dominican Republic can apply for a student visa, which allows them to stay in the country for the **duration of their studies**. This visa is typically valid for one year and can be extended as long as the individual remains enrolled in an accredited institution. Student visas are often the simplest to obtain for young people wishing to study in the country.

Working Visa

A working visa is required for individuals who plan to be employed by a company in the Dominican Republic. To apply for this visa, the employer must prove that the position cannot be filled by a local applicant. The **Dominican Republic Labor Law** governs the issuance of work permits and requires employers to apply on behalf of foreign workers. Once the working visa is approved, the employee can apply for **temporary residence**.

Tourist Visa with Extension

While not an ideal long-term solution, many people start their stay in the Dominican Republic on a **tourist visa**, which typically allows for a stay of up to 30 days, and **can be extended for another 30 days**. This option is popular for individuals who wish to explore the country before committing to a longer stay. However, staying in the country on a tourist visa for an extended period without switching to a proper long-term visa can lead to complications with immigration authorities.

Also keep in mind that while there's no specific **"digital nomad visa"** in the Dominican Republic, you can stay for up to 30 days with a **tourist visa**, and potentially extend it.

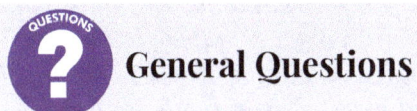

General Questions

1. *If I want to stay in the Dominican Republic for long-term and work, should I apply for a work permit before arriving in the Dominican Republic?* **Yes**. It's advisable to apply for a work permit **before** arriving in the Dominican Republic. You will need a job offer from a Dominican employer to apply. The employer must prove that the position can't be filled by a local. Once the permit is approved, you can apply for temporary residency, which allows you to work legally. Arriving without the permit can lead to legal issues, so it's best to have everything in place beforehand.

2. *I am American. Can I retire to the Dominican Republic?* **Yes**. Americans can retire in the Dominican Republic through the pensionado visa, which is designed for retirees with a regular income (e.g., pension or Social Security). You must show a minimum monthly income of US$1,500. This visa grants temporary residency, which can be extended and eventually converted into permanent residency. Retirees also enjoy benefits like discounts on utilities and medical services. The country's low cost of living and attractive lifestyle options make it a popular choice for U.S. retirees.

 ## Law of the Land Hypothetical

HYPOTHETICAL: *John, a U.S. citizen, moved to the Dominican Republic a few months ago on a tourist visa. He has been working remotely for his company in the U.S., earning a stable income. Initially, John thought he could just extend his tourist visa indefinitely, but now he's worried about the legal implications of overstaying his visa. He's heard about the Digital Nomad Visa and wonders if it applies to him and whether he can transition to it without leaving the country.*

ANSWER: *John should be cautious about overstaying his tourist visa, as doing so can result in fines or deportation. The Digital Nomad Visa is a good option for remote workers like him. He can apply for it while staying in the country, as long as he meets the income requirement of US$1,500 per month. The application process involves submitting proof of income and employment with a foreign company. Once approved, John can stay legally for a year, with the option to renew. To avoid issues, he should apply for the visa before his tourist visa expires.*

 ## Law of the Land True Story[46]

The Dominican Republic has become an increasingly popular destination for U.S. expats, retirees, and digital nomads seeking a warm climate, stunning beaches, and an affordable lifestyle. However, one often overlooked benefit of living abroad is the **Foreign Earned Income Exclusion (FEIE)**, a tax advantage for U.S. citizens living overseas.

As of 2024, the FEIE allows expats to exclude up to US$126,000 of earned income from U.S. taxation. To qualify, expats must meet either the Bonafide Residence or Physical Presence test. The **Bonafide Residence test** is met by being an official resident of a foreign country,

---

46 https://dominicantoday.com/dr/expats-corner/2024/06/05/
an-overlooked-tax-benefit-for-us-expats/

like the Dominican Republic. Alternatively, the **Physical Presence test** requires living outside the U.S. for 330 days within any 12-month period.

Only foreign-sourced earned income—such as wages for services performed abroad—qualifies for the exclusion, while passive income like rental income or dividends does not. For example, a U.S. citizen offering consulting services in the Dominican Republic could potentially exclude up to US$126,000 of their income from U.S. taxes. To claim the FEIE, expats must file **Form 2555**.

It's advisable for expats to consult a CPA or tax expert familiar with expatriate tax laws to ensure they fully understand and maximize their tax benefits while living abroad.

 **Takeaways**

- The Dominican Republic is a popular destination for U.S. expats, retirees, and digital nomads due to its warm climate, affordable living costs, beautiful landscapes, and ease of integration into the growing expat community.

- There are several visa options for long-term stays, including Residence Visas, Pensionado (retiree) Visas, Investor Visas, and Working Visas. Each has specific requirements, such as proving financial stability or meeting income thresholds, making it important for potential expats to choose the right option for their situation.

- U.S. expats living in the Dominican Republic can take advantage of the **Foreign Earned Income Exclusion** (**FEIE**), allowing them to exclude up to **US$126,000** of income from U.S. taxes, provided they meet either the **Bonafide Residence** or **Physical Presence** test. This can significantly reduce the tax burden for long-term residents.

- While the job market may not be as robust as in the U.S., there are opportunities in industries like tourism, hospitality, and teaching English. The rise of digital nomads is also notable, with remote workers increasingly choosing the Dominican Republic due to its affordable cost of living and solid internet infrastructure.

- The Dominican Republic boasts a growing and vibrant expat community, especially in major cities and popular beach towns. This sense of familiarity helps newcomers integrate more easily and find support from other foreign residents, making the transition to life in the country smoother.

CHAPTER 24
CIVIL LITIGATION

IN THIS CHAPTER

- Overview
- Personal Injury Claims and Compensation Law
- How to File a Civil Claim
- Service of Documents
- Statute of Limitations
- Getting Married in the Dominican Republic
- Law of the Land Hypothetical

CIVIL LITIGATION

Overview

Civil litigation provides a mechanism for resolving disputes, ensuring that travelers have a way to seek justice if legal issues arise while visiting another country. It helps them understand their rights and obligations under local laws, which may differ from those in their home country. The civil litigation system offers a formal process for addressing conflicts, such as contract disputes or personal injury claims, and can deter unfair practices by encouraging businesses to comply with legal standards. It also allows individuals to seek financial recourse for damages or losses and helps protect them from potential exploitation by local entities. Overall, understanding civil litigation enhances a visitor's experience and safety while traveling.

Personal Injury Claims and Compensation Law

Personal injury claims in the Dominican Republic aim to protect individuals who have suffered physical or psychological harm due to the actions or negligence of others. Compensation typically covers the **severity of the injury**, **medical expenses**, **lost wages**, and **emotional distress**. It is important for visitors to the Dominican Republic to understand their rights and the steps to take if they experience a personal injury while visiting.

Several types of personal injury claims in the Dominican Republic may qualify for compensation. These include **negligent security incidents**, such as assaults, robberies, and violent crimes on hotel and resort premises. Injuries due to **poorly maintained premises**, like slippery surfaces, balcony collapses, or unsafe amusement park rides, can also lead to claims. Additionally, **poisoning cases** involving tainted alcohol or unsafe substances may qualify for compensation.

After sustaining an injury in the Dominican Republic, the first priority is to ensure everyone is safe and receives **necessary medical care**. By law, you have to help the injured person; try to get them to a public hospital. It's also important to report the incident to the proper authorities and **obtain a police/incident report**. Documenting the accident scene, injuries, and witnesses by taking pictures can provide critical evidence. Moreover, it is important to **gather all pertinent information** about the accident as quickly as possible, including the date, time, weather conditions, and major factors leading up to the event.

In personal injury cases, attorneys use a formula to calculate **damages** and **financial losses**. The calculation begins with adding up all medical expenses resulting from the injury, known as "**special medical damages.**" All other damages, including social and emotional factors, are classified as "**general damages.**" Insurance adjusters may multiply the special medical damages by a factor of 1.5 to 5, depending on the injury's severity and painfulness. Awards for torts in the Dominican Republic are often **smaller compared to those in the U.S. or Britain**, with only compensatory damages being allowed.

In the Dominican Republic, mandatory insurance policies, such as third-party liability for motor vehicles, help cover the costs of accidents. Workers' compensation insurance can cover injuries sustained in the workplace, while health insurance may assist with medical expenses. If the responsible party has insurance, their coverage may also be tapped to settle the claim. In cases where the at-fault party is uninsured, the victim may need to rely on their own insurance policies, such as personal injury protection or uninsured motorist coverage.

Many law firms handle personal injury cases on a **contingency fee basis**, meaning that clients do not pay legal fees unless the attorney success-fully recovers compensation on their behalf. In such arrangements, the legal team advances all case-related costs and is only paid from a per-centage of the funds actually recovered. This percentage typically ranges from **20 to 35 percent**. Alternatively, some lawyers charge hourly fees or fixed rates for specific legal services. It's essential to clarify the fee struc-ture with a lawyer before engaging their services to avoid any surprises.

To find a qualified personal injury attorney in the Dominican Republic, start by seeking recommendations from trusted locals or colleagues who may have personal experiences with lawyers. You can also consult the **Colegio de Abogados de la República Dominicana** (**Dominican Bar Association**) for a directory of licensed attorneys. Online platforms like **AbogadosRD.com** or **hg.org** offer lists of lawyers specializing in per-sonal injury cases. It is important to act promptly, as time bars for bring-ing a lawsuit can run as short as six months to no more than two years from the date of the incident.

How to File a Civil Claim

Filing a civil claim in the Dominican Republic involves several key steps and requires attention to specific legal procedures. First, you must en-sure that you have **legal standing** to file the claim, meaning you must be personally or financially affected by the matter. You also need to be aware of the **statute of limitations**, which sets deadlines for filing cer-tain claims, depending on the nature of the case. Civil claims can involve a variety of issues, such as contract disputes, tort claims like personal injury, family law matters, property disputes, debt collection, and labor claims. For each case, you'll need to provide key documents, including identification (national ID card or passport for foreigners), a signed power of attorney if represented by a lawyer, a formal written complaint detailing the facts of your case, evidence to support your claim (such as contracts, medical reports, photographs, or witness statements), and payment of the required court fees.

Civil claims are typically filed in the **First Instance Court** (*Tribunal de Primera Instancia*), which is determined by factors such as the nature of the claim and the geographical location of the event or the defendant. For instance, a property dispute would generally be filed in the civil courts, while family law issues might be handled in specialized family courts. Depending on the complexity and value of the claim, higher courts, such as the **Court of Appeals** (*Tribunal de Apelación*) or even the **Supreme Court** (*Corte Suprema de Justicia*), may become involved if an appeal or further review is necessary. It's essential to consult with a qualified local lawyer who can guide you through the process and help ensure that all necessary legal requirements and deadlines are met.

The process of filing a civil claim in the Dominican Republic can differ for visitors versus residents, primarily due to the legal standing and procedural requirements for each group. For **residents**, filing a civil claim is generally more straightforward. Residents are considered to have legal standing in the Dominican Republic and can directly file claims without needing special authorization. They can use their national identification card (or residency documents if they are foreigners) to prove their identity and eligibility to file. Residents are also more familiar with the local legal system and the court processes, which can make navigating the system easier. Additionally, residents can use local addresses for official communications, which ensures that any legal notices or court documents are properly delivered.

For **visitors** (i.e., individuals who are temporarily in the country without long-term residence status), the process can be more complicated. While visitors have the right to file a civil claim, they may need to provide **additional documentation**. They must present their passport and, in some cases, a temporary residence permit if they are staying in the country for an extended period. A visitor may also need to designate a **legal representative** (a lawyer with power of attorney) in the Dominican Republic to act on their behalf, especially if they are unable to attend hearings or if there are communication difficulties due to language or location barriers. In addition, visitors may need to ensure they have a **local address for service of process**, or their lawyer will receive notifications on their behalf.

Another notable difference is related to the **enforcement of judgments**. For residents, enforcing a court decision (e.g., collecting compensation or ensuring compliance) is generally more straightforward, as they are within the country and subject to local jurisdiction. For visitors, if the defendant is in the Dominican Republic, enforcement is still relatively direct. However, if the person or entity responsible for the claim is outside of the country, enforcing a judgment may require **international legal procedures**, which can be more complicated and time-consuming.

Service of Documents[47]

In the Dominican Republic, the service of process is a critical aspect of the legal system, ensuring that parties involved in a case are properly notified. The rules governing the service of documents are outlined in the country's **Code of Civil Procedure**. The primary objective is to provide individuals or entities with clear notice of legal actions that affect them. Service can be executed using various methods such as **personal service**, where documents are handed directly to the individual, substitute service, where documents are left with a family member or representative, or **public notice**, which involves publishing the notice in a local newspaper if the person cannot be located. Registered mail can also be used, though it is typically less common for initiating formal legal proceedings.

In the Dominican Republic, the responsibility for serving legal documents usually falls on a **court-appointed process server** or the **attorney representing the party filing the claim**. The process server is responsible for delivering the documents in person or through other authorized means, ensuring compliance with the legal requirements. Once the service is carried out, **proof of service** must be documented in a certificate of service, which includes details like the name of the person served, the method, and the date and time of service. This certificate is then submitted to the court to confirm that the defendant or party was properly notified.

---

47 https://www.dgrlegal.com/
    international-service-of-process-in-the-dominican-republic/

For visitors in the Dominican Republic, the service of process is slightly more complicated. Visitors may not have a local address, which means a lawyer or a process server will need to locate them through their temporary accommodations or other means. If direct service is not possible, **substitute service** or **service by public notice** may be used. Visitors are typically required to appoint a **local legal representative** who can accept service on their behalf, especially if they are not present in the country for the duration of the case. This legal representative would handle the case and any legal documents in the visitor's absence, ensuring the process continues without delay.

Statute of Limitations

In the Dominican Republic, the statute of limitations governs the period within which a party must initiate a civil lawsuit. Once this time period expires, the claim is typically no longer valid, and the right to bring the lawsuit is lost. The **Code of Civil Procedure** (*Código de Procedimiento Civil*) outlines the various time limits for filing civil suits, and these periods can vary depending on the type of claim. Generally, the statute of limitations for civil suits in the Dominican Republic is designed to promote legal certainty and prevent stale claims from being pursued after evidence and witnesses may no longer be reliable.

For most civil claims, the statute of limitations in the Dominican Republic is **10 years**. This period applies to a broad range of civil matters, such as **property disputes** and **contract claims**. However, specific types of claims may have different timeframes. For example, in cases of **personal injury**, the statute of limitations is typically **three years** from the date of the injury or the moment when the injury was discovered, whichever occurs later. **Claims involving commercial debts** or other financial obligations might have a **six-year statute of limitations**. For claims related to **contracts**, the limit is generally **10 years**, but for **bills of exchange** or **promissory notes**, it can be as short as **three years**. In family law cases, such as **divorce or child custody claims**, the statute of limitations may vary depending on the specific nature of the claim, though it tends to be **one to five years** for matters like child support or alimony disputes.

Several factors can influence the length of the statute of limitations, including the nature of the claim, the parties involved, and any special legal circumstances that may apply. For example, if a party is incapacitated or out of the country, the statute of limitations may be temporarily suspended, allowing the time limit to be extended. This is often referred to as "**suspension**" or "**interruption**" of the statute of limitations, where the period during which a party cannot act due to illness, travel, or legal incapacity does not count against the total time allowed for filing a claim. Additionally, if the defendant engages in certain actions, such as fraud or other deceptive conduct that prevents the claimant from discovering the facts underlying the claim, the statute of limitations may be **extended** or **postponed** until the claimant reasonably discovers the cause of action.

If a civil suit is filed after the statute of limitations has expired, the defendant has the right to request the dismissal of the case based on the expiration of the statute of limitations. In practice, once the statute of limitations has passed, the court will generally **reject the claim**, as the time for legal action has expired. However, in some instances, the court may choose to examine whether any exceptional circumstances apply that might justify an extension or tolling of the statute of limitations. If the claim is dismissed due to the expiration of the statute, the claimant loses the opportunity to seek judicial relief for that particular matter.

 **Getting Married in the Dominican Republic**

Getting married in the Dominican Republic is a straightforward process, whether you're a resident, foreigner, or Dominican national. While the process is relatively simple, it's important to be aware of the legal requirements, documentation, and specific steps involved to ensure that your marriage is valid both in the Dominican Republic and internationally.

In the Dominican Republic, the legal requirements for marriage are relatively clear. Both parties must be at least **18 years old**. If either party is between 16 and 18 years old, parental consent is required.

Additionally, both individuals must be mentally sound and not already married. Marriages in the Dominican Republic are governed by the Civil Code, which ensures that all marriages are legally binding once registered.

To apply for a marriage license in the Dominican Republic, you will need to provide the following documents:

- **Valid Passport or National ID Card** (for Dominican nationals).

- **Birth Certificate** (a copy of the birth certificate for both parties, which must be legalized or apostilled if issued outside the Dominican Republic).

- **Certificate of No Impediment to Marriage** (this is a document stating that there are no legal obstacles preventing the marriage, which is typically required for foreign nationals. Some countries provide this certificate, while others may require an affidavit).

- **Divorce or Widowhood Certificate** (if applicable, for either party who was previously married).

- **Proof of Residency** (for foreigners residing in the Dominican Republic, a document showing residency or a tourist visa if applicable).

These documents must be translated into Spanish if they are in another language and, in many cases, must be notarized or legalized.

To obtain a marriage license in the Dominican Republic, both parties must apply at the **Civil Registry Office** (*Oficialía Civil*). The process involves submitting the required documents and paying the associated fees. The couple will be asked to complete a marriage application, and the civil registry office will verify the documents. In some cases, an interview may be required. Once the paperwork is processed, the couple can proceed to marry. The process can take anywhere from **two to four business days** to complete, depending on the complexity of the documents and whether additional steps, such as notarization or translation, are needed. If there are no issues with the documents, the process is relatively fast, and the couple can typically marry within the same week.

There are **no strict residency requirements** for foreign nationals who wish to get married in the Dominican Republic. Even tourists can get married in the country, provided they meet the legal documentation requirements. However, foreign nationals must ensure that they have the correct paperwork, including a valid passport and a certificate of no impediment to marriage. It is also important to note that foreign nationals will need to have their marriage registered with the appropriate authorities in their home country for international recognition.

A **civil ceremony** in the Dominican Republic is the most common and legally recognized form of marriage. It is performed by a judge or a notary public at the Civil Registry Office. This ceremony is legally binding as long as it is registered with the civil authorities. The process is simple, with no religious affiliation required. A **religious ceremony** can be held after the civil ceremony if the couple desires a religious service. However, for the marriage to be legally recognized in the Dominican Republic, it must first be registered civilly. The religious ceremony may be performed by a priest or religious leader, but this does not automatically confer legal status to the marriage unless it is also registered with the civil authorities.

The fees for getting married in the Dominican Republic are relatively low. The cost for obtaining a marriage license typically ranges from **RD$1,000-3,000** (approximately **US$20-60**). The cost of the civil ceremony itself is often included in the marriage license fee, but additional fees may apply if you choose to have the ceremony at a location other than the registry office or if you require a notary or judge to officiate. Religious ceremonies, if separate from the civil procedure, may involve additional costs, such as donations to the church or fees for the officiant.

After the civil ceremony is conducted, the marriage is officially registered in the **Civil Registry**. The couple will receive a **Marriage Certificate** (*Acta de Matrimonio*), which serves as proof of their legal marriage in the Dominican Republic. This certificate is necessary for obtaining a marriage record and for international recognition of the marriage. If the couple is from abroad, the marriage certificate can be legalized or apostilled for use in their home country.

The marriages taking place in the Dominican Republic are generally **recognized internationally**, especially in countries that have signed international treaties or conventions on the matter. The marriage must be registered with the local authorities and a certified copy of the marriage certificate must be obtained. If needed, the marriage certificate can be **apostilled** or **legalized** by the Dominican Ministry of Foreign Affairs to ensure its recognition abroad. Some countries may have specific requirements for recognizing foreign marriages, so it is important to consult with the local embassy or consulate to ensure that the marriage will be recognized in the couple's home country.

Law of the Land Hypothetical

HYPOTHETICAL: *Carlos, a foreign national from the United States, has been living in the Dominican Republic for two years as an expatirate. While at a market, he slipped on a wet floor and injured his back, requiring treatment and physical therapy. His medical bills have increased, and he had to take time off work. Carlos wants to file a personal injury lawsuit against the market.*

What is the statute of limitations for Carlos to file a personal injury claim in the Dominican Republic, and are there any special considerations since he is a foreign national?

ANSWER: *In the Dominican Republic, the statute of limitations for personal injury claims is three years from the date of the injury or its discovery, so Carlos has three years from the day of the accident to file his claim. As a foreign national, Carlos doesn't face special restrictions regarding the filing period. However, he will need to provide proof of legal stay (such as a visa or work permit) when filing. Additionally, Carlos must hire a Dominican lawyer to represent him, as the proceedings will be in Spanish and follow local laws. If Carlos is outside the country when the lawsuit is filed, a process server may be used to notify him of legal actions, but this won't extend the statute of limitations.*

OTHER THINGS TO KNOW

IN THIS CHAPTER

- Tourists and Street Hustling
- Safety Concerns and Practical Tips
- In the Event of Death
- Experiencing Financial Hardship

OTHER THINGS TO KNOW

Tourists and Street Hustling[48]

In the Dominican Republic, street hustling is a **common issue in tourist-heavy areas**, where individuals aggressively offer goods or services to visitors. These hustlers often use tactics that involve high-pressure sales or deceptive practices to make a quick sale. The goods and services typically offered by street hustlers include **souvenirs** such as jewelry, T-shirts, and local crafts, which are often sold at inflated prices. Tourists may be led to believe they're getting a good deal, but later realize the prices are much higher than standard rates. Additionally, hustlers frequently offer **unlicensed taxis or tours**, often at seemingly attractive prices, only for tourists to end up paying much more than originally agreed. Street performers might approach tourists, offering to take their photos or perform for them, and then demand an inflated fee after the service. In some cases, street vendors sell **food or drinks at exorbitant prices**, sometimes without providing receipts or charging more than what's customary.

Street hustling is most prevalent in areas with heavy tourist traffic. **Punta Cana**, a popular resort destination, is known for its beach areas and all-inclusive hotels, making it a hotspot for hustlers. In Santo Domingo, the **Colonial Zone**, with its historical and cultural attractions, also sees

---

48 https://kasventures.wordpress.com/2022/02/01/
    dominican-republic-scams/

a significant amount of street hustling. **Puerto Plata's Malecon** area and other tourist spots are known for unlicensed taxis and unsolicited services, and towns like **Sosúa** and **Cabarete**, popular with expats and backpackers, also experience a high level of street hustling activity.

Tourists should be cautious of several **common scams**. One of the most frequent scams is the **"free gift" scam**, where a hustler offers a "free" gift, such as a bracelet or necklace, only to demand a large payment once the item is in the tourist's hands. Another common scam is the **"taxi" scam**, where an unofficial taxi driver offers a ride at a low rate but later demands much more than agreed or takes unnecessary detours to increase the fare. The **photo scam** also occurs frequently, where individuals offer to take pictures of tourists and then demand a high fee afterward. In addition, tourists may encounter **fake charity requests**, where hustlers pose as charity workers asking for donations for non-existent causes.

Local authorities and tourism organizations are aware of the issue of street hustling and have taken steps to address it. The Dominican Republic's **Tourism Police**, or *Cuerpo Especializado de Seguridad Turística (CESTUR)*, actively patrol popular tourist areas, attempting to control aggressive selling and unlicensed operations. Their presence is especially noticeable in areas like Punta Cana and Santo Domingo, where street hustling is more common. The **Ministry of Tourism** has also launched **awareness campaigns** to inform visitors about potential scams and encourage them to report any suspicious behavior. While these efforts have helped reduce some instances of street hustling, the practice remains a challenge, especially in crowded tourist zones. Tourists are advised to stay vigilant, avoid engaging with persistent hustlers, and report any issues to local authorities.

Safety Concerns and Practical Tips

Interacting with street hustlers in the Dominican Republic can pose a range of safety concerns, primarily due to aggressive or deceptive behavior. Some hustlers may become confrontational if they feel a tourist is not willing to purchase their goods or services, which can lead to verbal or even physical altercations. In addition to the physical safety risks, tourists may also fall victim to scams, which can result in financial loss. Some hustlers may offer to guide tourists to certain attractions or provide services like transportation, only to overcharge them or leave them stranded in unsafe areas.

To protect themselves from aggressive hustlers, tourists should remain **calm and assertive** when dealing with persistent vendors. It is wise to politely but firmly decline any unsolicited offers, avoiding engaging in prolonged conversations or negotiating with individuals who approach them in tourist areas. Tourists should **always agree on prices upfront** if they decide to purchase goods or services and ensure that they are fully aware of any hidden costs. Using **reputable transportation services** and avoiding unofficial taxis or tour guides can also prevent potential scams. It's important to **avoid carrying large amounts of cash** in visible areas and to keep valuables securely stored, as hustlers often target those who appear distracted or overly confident with their belongings.

Local customs and behaviors that can help tourists navigate street interactions include maintaining a polite yet firm demeanor when interacting with vendors or hustlers. Smiling and nodding politely while declining an offer without further engagement is often enough to signal that the individual is not interested. In the Dominican Republic, it is not uncommon for people to approach tourists in a friendly manner, but tourists should remain cautious and be aware of their surroundings at all times. Understanding basic Spanish phrases, such as *"No, gracias"* (No, thank you), can also help in these situations, as many hustlers may rely on language barriers to manipulate tourists into paying for services they didn't request.

If tourists experience harassment, feel threatened, or become victims of scams, there are several resources available to report the incident. The **Tourism Police**, which is specifically tasked with ensuring the safety of tourists, can be contacted in popular tourist zones. The police have a presence in areas like Punta Cana, Santo Domingo, and Puerto Plata. Additionally, tourists can contact the **Dominican Republic Ministry of Tourism**, which operates a tourist helpline and offers support in addressing complaints related to scams or harassment. Many hotels and resorts also provide assistance in reporting any incidents and may help coordinate with the authorities. Tourists are encouraged to document any incidents, take note of descriptions or license plate numbers if applicable, and report the situation as soon as possible to prevent further issues.

 ## In the Event of Death[49]

In the unfortunate event that someone traveling with you dies while in the Dominican Republic, there are several important steps to take to ensure that legal, logistical, and emotional matters are handled properly. First, you should immediately **contact local authorities**. In most cases, the **National Police** (*Policía Nacional*) should be notified to report the death, particularly if it occurs under unexpected or suspicious circumstances. They will initiate an investigation and will be the point of contact for any further questions regarding the cause of death.

Next, you should contact your **embassy or consulate** as soon as possible. The embassy can assist with a variety of matters, including offering guidance on local procedures, helping you navigate communication with the Dominican authorities, and offering support with repatriation. Embassies also help with notifying the deceased's family, if necessary, and may facilitate communication between you and funeral homes or other necessary services. They will also guide you through the legalities of obtaining the proper documentation to move forward, such as a **death certificate**.

Handling the deceased's remains is another crucial matter. Once the police and authorities have been notified and an official report has been made, the next step is working with a **funeral home** or **embalming service** in the Dominican Republic. These services will handle the preparation of the body for either local burial or repatriation. The funeral home will also assist with obtaining the **death certificate**, which is required

---

49 https://travel.state.gov/content/travel/en/international-travel/while-abroad/death-abroad1/return-of-remains-of-deceased-us-citizen.html

for transporting the body. Keep in mind that there are certain regulations regarding embalming and the paperwork required for transporting the remains internationally.

Bringing the body home involves working with both the Dominican funeral service and a funeral home in the deceased's home country, which may handle the final transportation. This process can be lengthy and costly, and it will require the proper paperwork, including the death certificate, embalming certification, and any additional documents that may be required by the country receiving the remains. You should expect to work with the consulate or embassy to arrange for the required documentation and permits. Additionally, some countries may require an autopsy or other formal investigations if the death was unexpected.

Family members should be aware that repatriation of remains can be a complex process, often requiring several days to complete. It's essential to stay in contact with the embassy, funeral homes, and relevant authorities to ensure that everything is handled efficiently. The family may also want to inquire about **local insurance coverage**, as certain travel insurance policies may provide assistance with the costs of repatriating remains, including transportation and preparation fees.

Ultimately, handling the death of a loved one in a foreign country is a distressing experience, but local authorities, the embassy, and funeral services are there to help navigate the process, provide support, and ensure that the deceased's remains are treated with respect and dignity.

Experiencing Financial Hardship

Traveling in the Dominican Republic can be an exciting experience, but it can also bring unexpected financial challenges. If you find yourself facing financial hardship while visiting, there are several reasons why this might occur, as well as ways to manage and find support.

One of the most common reasons tourists might face financial hardship is due to **currency exchange issues**. The local currency, the Dominican Peso (DOP), is used for most transactions, although US dollars (USD) are widely accepted in tourist areas. However, not understanding the exchange rate or over-relying on USD can lead to overspending. Additionally, tourists may encounter **unexpected emergencies** such as medical issues, accidents, or the need for last-minute flight changes, all of which can result in unplanned expenses. Another common issue is the **high markup of goods and services** in tourist hotspots, where prices are often inflated compared to local areas. Many tourists also experience financial strain due to high fees on ATM withdrawals, poor exchange rates, or the tendency to overestimate how much they can afford to spend without budgeting properly.

If you do find yourself in a situation where you have run out of money, there are several steps you can take. First, **contact your embassy or consulate** for emergency assistance. They may offer emergency loans or help arrange for money to be sent from home. Alternatively, **reaching out to family or friends** back home who can wire money via services like **Western Union, MoneyGram**, or **Remitly** can be a quick and effective way to get the help you need. If you have a credit or debit card, you can use it to withdraw cash or make payments, though be sure to check for any international transaction fees. Some hotels and local businesses may also offer payment plans, so it's worth asking if they are willing to work with you if you're unable to pay immediately. Additionally, some local banks, like Banco Popular or Scotiabank, offer services that can help with international transfers.

If you find yourself in a financial bind, **budgeting** can help stretch the money you do have. Prioritize essentials such as food, shelter, and transportation. Consider opting for local eateries and markets instead of dining at tourist spots, as this can save you a significant amount of money. Public transportation, such as buses or shared taxis, is often much cheaper than private taxis or resort transfers. Look for **free or low-cost activities**, such as visiting public parks, exploring local beaches, or enjoying cultural events that don't require an entrance fee. If you're staying in a place with a shared kitchen, buying groceries and preparing your meals can save you a lot compared to eating out every day. Finally, it's always a good idea to **set aside some emergency funds** for unexpected situations, as this can provide peace of mind and prevent further financial strain.

QUICK REFERENCE GUIDE

- Quick Chapter References to Important Topics

QUICK REFERENCE GUIDE

Crime in the Dominican Republic

Are there particular areas I should avoid as a tourist?

Yes. While the Dominican Republic is generally safe for tourists, there are areas that can be more prone to crime or safety risks. In **Santo Domingo**, neighborhoods like Capotillo and San Carlos should be avoided, especially at night. In **Puerto Plata**, areas like La Ceiba and Montellano may also have higher crime rates. Some parts of **La Romana** and **Santiago**, such as El Higuero and Cienfuegos, can be less tourist-friendly. Rural areas near the Haitian border or remote mountain regions should be approached with caution due to limited infrastructure and occasional tensions. To stay safe, stick to well-lit, busy tourist zones, avoid secluded beaches after dark, and use reliable transportation like reputable taxis or ride-sharing services. *For more details, see Chapter 3.*

Drug Offenses

Is the possession of marijuana legal?

No. The possession of marijuana is **illegal** in the Dominican Republic. While there have been discussions around decriminalization, marijuana is still prohibited for recreational use, and possession can lead to legal consequences such as fines, arrest, or imprisonment.

Is the possession of cocaine legal?

> **No.** The possession of cocaine is **illegal** in the Dominican Republic. It is considered a serious crime, and being caught with cocaine can result in severe penalties, including long prison sentences and heavy fines. Foreign nationals caught with cocaine can also face deportation. *For more details, see Chapter 4.*

Alcohol-Related Offenses

What is the legal drinking age?

> The legal drinking age in the Dominican Republic is **18 years old**. Individuals must be at least 18 to purchase and consume alcoholic beverages.

What is the legal blood alcohol limit to drive?

> In the Dominican Republic, the legal blood alcohol concentration (BAC) limit for **drivers** is **0.05 percent**. For **professional drivers**, the BAC limit is **0.00 percent** (zero tolerance), while for **motorcycle drivers**, the BAC limit is **0.02 percent**. *For more details, see Chapter 5.*

Firearm & Ammunition Offenses

Can I possess a gun?

> **Yes.** You can possess a gun in the Dominican Republic, but you must obtain a legal firearm license. To do so, you need to be at least **21 years old**, have a clean criminal record, and pass psychological and physical evaluations. You must also demonstrate a legitimate need for the firearm, such as for self-defense or hunting, and go through an approval process with the Ministry of the Interior and Police.

Can I possess ammunition?

> **Yes.** You can possess ammunition, but only if you hold a legal firearm license. Ammunition possession is tied to firearm ownership, and it is illegal to possess ammunition without a registered firearm. Ammunition is sold under strict regulations, and unauthorized

possession can lead to legal consequences. *For more details, see Chapter 6.*

Prostitution

Is prostitution legal?

Yes. Prostitution is legal in the Dominican Republic. However, while selling sex is not criminalized, there are regulations in place to prevent exploitation and abuse. It is illegal to engage in human trafficking, the exploitation of minors, or to coerce individuals into prostitution. Brothels or establishments where prostitution is organized are illegal, and soliciting on public streets is also subject to local laws and regulations. Prostitution is tolerated, but any form of exploitation or illegal activity related to it is punishable by law. *For more details, see Chapter 7.*

LGBTQ

Is homosexuality legal?

Yes. Homosexuality is **legal** in the Dominican Republic. There are no laws that criminalize same-sex sexual activity between consenting adults.

Are same-sex public displays of affection legal and socially acceptable?

No. Same-sex public displays of affection are not widely accepted in the Dominican Republic. While homosexuality is legal, public displays of affection between same-sex couples may face social disapproval and could lead to uncomfortable or negative reactions in more conservative areas. The country is generally considered more conservative regarding LGBTQ+ rights, and social acceptance of public same-sex affection is still evolving. *For more details, see Chapter 8.*

Arrested in the Dominican Republic

Would I be entitled to bail if I'm arrested?

Yes. You may be entitled to bail if arrested in the Dominican Republic, but it depends on the charges and the circumstances of the case. For minor offenses, bail is more likely to be granted, while for more serious crimes, bail may be denied or set at a higher amount. The judge will decide based on the specifics of the case, including the likelihood of the accused fleeing or committing further crimes.

Will a lawyer be provided to me if I cannot afford one?

Yes. If you are arrested or detained in the Dominican Republic and cannot afford a lawyer, the Dominican government must provide you with a public defender, ensuring you have the right to legal representation. *For more details, see Chapter 10.*

Helping a Friend or Relative Imprisoned in the Dominican Republic

Can I send money to a friend or relative imprisoned in the Dominican Republic?

Yes. You can send money to a friend or family member who is imprisoned in the Dominican Republic. There are official channels, such as prison administration services, through which funds can be deposited into an inmate's account. However, it is important to follow the specific procedures and regulations set by the prison or correctional facility, as there may be limitations on the amount or method of transfer.

Can I remain in the country upon release from prison or jail after my sentence is complete?

Yes. You can remain in the Dominican Republic after completing your sentence, provided you have the legal right to stay in the country. If you are a foreign national, your legal status will be determined by immigration laws. Upon release, if your visa or residency status is still valid, you can stay. However, if your status has expired, you may need to regularize it with immigration authorities. If you were deported or have a criminal record, there may be restrictions on re-entry. *For more details, see Chapter 12.*

Crime Victim Assistance

Can a victim of a crime be legally compensated?

Yes. A victim of a crime in the Dominican Republic can be legally compensated, but the process depends on the nature of the crime and the circumstances. In cases of personal injury or damage caused by criminal acts, victims may be entitled to compensation through civil claims or as part of the criminal prosecution. This may involve seeking restitution from the offender, although the process can be complex, and legal assistance is often required.

How can a foreigner in the Dominican Republic report a crime they are a victim of?

To report a crime as a foreigner in the Dominican Republic, you should go to the nearest police station (Comisión de la Policía Nacional) to file a report. It is advisable to bring identification documents (passport, residency permit, etc.) and provide details about the crime. For emergencies, you can also contact the **National Emergency Number 911.** If you are unable to speak Spanish, it may be helpful to have an interpreter, as not all police officers may speak English. You can also contact your embassy or consulate for further assistance. *For more details, see Chapter 14.*

U.S. Consulate Assistance

Are there any limitations to the consulate assistance I can receive while in the Dominican Republic?

Yes. Consulate assistance in the Dominican Republic is available but has limitations. The consulate cannot provide legal representation, pay fines, or intervene directly in legal matters. They can offer legal guidance and help ensure your rights are respected but cannot influence the outcome of criminal proceedings or secure your release. If you lose your passport, the consulate can issue an emergency one, but there may be delays. They cannot guarantee safety or prevent deportation if local laws or immigration rules have been violated. *For more details, see Chapter 14.*

Police

Is there an official police force?

Yes. The Dominican Republic has an official police force known as the **National Police** (*Policía Nacional*). It is responsible for maintaining public order, preventing and investigating crimes, and enforcing the law throughout the country. The National Police operates under the Ministry of the Interior and Police, and it is the primary law enforcement agency in the Dominican Republic. *For more details, see Chapter 15.*

How to Get Legal Help in the Dominican Republic

Is there a resource in the Dominican Republic to find legal representation?

Yes. In the Dominican Republic, there are resources to help you find legal representation. You can contact the **Dominican Bar Association** (*Colegio de Abogados de la República Dominicana*), which maintains a directory of licensed attorneys. Additionally, many law firms in major cities offer legal services, and some specialize in assisting foreigners.

Is there free legal representation assistance?

Yes. There is some access to free legal representation, but it is limited. The government provides legal aid through public defenders in criminal cases, but these services are generally not as readily available for civil matters. Free legal assistance may also be available through non-governmental organizations, but it depends on the case and availability of resources.

Does my home country's embassy provide a list of local attorneys?

Yes. Most countries maintain a list of local attorneys through their embassy or consulate. While the embassy may not directly recommend specific lawyers, they typically provide a list of licensed attorneys who can assist you. Some of these lawyers may speak English or other languages, depending on the embassy's resources and the local legal community. *For more details, see Chapter 16.*

Foreign Embassies in the Dominican Republic

Are there foreign embassies in the Dominican Republic?

Yes. There are foreign embassies in the Dominican Republic. Many countries have established embassies or consulates in the capital, Santo Domingo, to assist their citizens with consular services, including legal assistance, passport issues, and emergency support.

Is there a website to locate embassies in the Dominican Republic?

Yes. You can locate embassies in the Dominican Republic through various online resources. One option is the official website of the **Ministry of Foreign Affairs of the Dominican Republic** (*Ministerio de Relaciones Exteriores*), which provides a list of foreign embassies and consulates in the country. Additionally, many embassies maintain their own websites with contact information and services available to their nationals. *For more details, see Chapter 16.*

Medical Facilities & Hospitals

Is there a number I can call for ambulance and fire emergencies?

Yes. In the Dominican Republic, you can call **911** for both ambulance and fire emergencies. The emergency number is available nationwide, and it is the primary number to reach emergency services, including medical assistance and fire departments.

If I am injured while on vacation in the Dominican Republic, are there hospitals that are recommended for tourists?

Yes. There are several hospitals in the Dominican Republic that are recommended for tourists, particularly in larger cities like Santo Domingo and Punta Cana. Some of the well-known hospitals include **Centro de Medicina Avanzada (CMA)** in Santo Domingo, **Hospital General de la Plaza de la Salud**, and **Hospital Dr. Bournigal** in Puerto Plata. These hospitals are equipped with modern medical facilities and are accustomed to handling medical emergencies involving foreigners. It's advisable to contact your embassy for additional recommendations and assistance in case of a medical emergency. *For more details, see Chapter 17.*

Driving in the Dominican Republic

Which side of the road do I drive on?

You drive on the **right side** of the road in the Dominican Republic.

Can I use my driver's license from my home country to drive in the Dominican Republic?

Yes. You can use your driver's license from your home country to drive in the Dominican Republic for a short period (usually **up to 30 days**). However, it's often recommended to carry an **International Driving Permit (IDP)** along with your home country license, especially if it's not in Spanish, to avoid language barriers with local authorities.

How old do I need to be to rent a car?

To rent a car, you generally need to be at least **21 years old**. Some rental agencies may require you to be 25, particularly for larger vehicles, and may impose additional fees for drivers under 25. You will also need a valid driver's license and a credit card. *For more details, see Chapter 18.*

Nude Beaches & Clothing-Optional Resorts

Is public nudity legal on the beaches?

No. Public nudity is **not legal** on the beaches of the Dominican Republic. While the country has many beautiful beaches, nudity is generally prohibited in public spaces. Some private resorts or designated areas may have more relaxed rules, but outside of those, it's important to follow local norms and dress appropriately in public areas. Violating these rules could result in fines or other penalties. *For more details, see Chapter 19.*

Tourist Taxation

Is there room tax in the Dominican Republic?

Yes. In the Dominican Republic, the room tax, known as **ITBIS** (*Impuesto a la Transferencia de Bienes Industrializados y Servicios*), is an **18 percent value-added tax** on hotel room rentals and other services. The tax is collected from the guest and paid to the tax authorities by the accommodation provider.

Is there any fee associated with leaving the Dominican Republic?

Yes. There's a **US$20 departure tax** when leaving the Dominican Republic, which is usually included in your airfare, but you should verify with your airline. If not included, you will have to pay it at the airport when leaving. This tax is required for all passengers leaving the Dominican Republic by air. *For more details, see Chapter 22.*

Long-Term Stays

Do I need to return to my home country to apply for a work permit in the Dominican Republic?

No. You do not need to return to your home country to apply for a work permit in the Dominican Republic. You can apply for a work permit from within the country. To do so, you would typically need to secure a job offer from a Dominican employer who can sponsor your application. The employer will submit the necessary documents to the Dominican Ministry of Labor and immigration authorities to process the work permit.

As an American, how long can I stay in the Dominican Republic without a visa?

As an American, you can stay in the Dominican Republic without a visa for **up to 30 days as a tourist**. This period can be extended once for an **additional 30 days** by applying at the Dominican immigration office, allowing a **total stay of up to 60 days without a visa**. After this, you would need to leave the country or apply for an extension or residency if you wish to stay longer. *For more details, see Chapter 23.*

In the Event of Death

What documents would an embassy need regarding the death of a tourist?

In the event of a tourist's death in the Dominican Republic, the embassy typically requires the **death certificate** issued by local authorities or the hospital, along with the deceased's **identification documents** like a passport or national ID. A **consular report of death** is also needed to officially record the death. The embassy will ask for **contact information of the next of kin** to help coordinate repatriation or burial arrangements. If applicable, **travel and insurance details** will be required to assist with the return of the body and related expenses. If the death is suspicious or involves an accident, a **police report** may be needed to clarify the circumstances. The embassy's role is to guide the family through the process and assist with local arrangements. *For more details, see Chapter 25.*

EMERGENCY/IMPORTANT CONTACT NUMBERS IN THE DOMINICAN REPUBLIC

 Please consider putting some of these numbers in your phone **prior** to traveling to the Dominican Republic.

Emergency Numbers:

- **Police:** 809-686-8227
- **Fire:** 809-682-5777
- **Ambulance:** 809-682-5777 or 911 (National Emergency Number)

Other Useful Contacts:

- **General Emergency Services:** 911
- **Medical Assistance:** 849-451-1490 (also available via WhatsApp)
- **Tourist Police (outside Santo Domingo):** 809-200-3500
- **Coast Guard:** 809-200-0370
- **Roadside Assistance:** 809-544-4444
- **VIDA Line (Gender-Based Violence Support):** 212 or 809-200-7212

Legal Assistance:

- **Dominican Bar Association:** 809-332-1111
- **Legal Aid:** Available through public defenders, or you can contact a local attorney from the Dominican Bar Association.
- **U.S. Embassy in the Dominican Republic:** +(809) 567-7775, SDOamericans@state.gov

USEFUL SPANISH PHRASES

Greetings

HI/HELLO – Hola

GOOD MORNING – Buenos días

GOOD AFTERNOON – Buenas tardes

GOOD NIGHT – Buenas noches

GOODBYE – Adiós

Magic Words

PLEASE – Por favor

THANK YOU – Gracias

YOU'RE WELCOME – De nada

CHEERS! – ¡Salud!

EXCUSE ME – Disculpe / Perdón

Getting Around

WHERE IS THE BATHROOM? – ¿Dónde está el baño?

WHAT TIME IS IT? – ¿Qué hora es?

HOW DO I GET TO…? – ¿Cómo llego a …?

WHERE DOES THIS TRAIN/BUS GO? – ¿Dónde va este tren/autobús?

RESTAURANT – Restaurante

HOW MUCH DOES THIS COST? – ¿Cuánto cuesta esto?

TRAIN/METRO STATION – Estación de tren/metro

Communication

DO YOU SPEAK ENGLISH? – ¿Habla inglés?

I DO NOT UNDERSTAND – No entiendo

I DON'T SPEAK (COUNTRY'S LANGUAGE) – No hablo español

I DON'T KNOW – No sé

Emergency

HELP! – ¡Ayuda!

CALL AN AMBULANCE! – ¡Llame a una ambulancia!

I NEED A DOCTOR – Necesito un doctor

POLICE – Policía

I'M LOST – Estoy perdido/a

IT'S AN EMERGENCY – Es una emergencia

GLOSSARY

ACQUITTAL: A jury verdict that a criminal defendant is not guilty, or the finding of a judge that the evidence cannot support a conviction.

ADVERSARY PROCEEDING: A lawsuit arising from a controversy that begins with filing a complaint.

AFFIDAVIT: A written statement made under oath.

APPEAL: A request made after a trial court has decided against one party in which the losing party asks a higher court to review the decision for legal error.

ARRAIGNMENT: A proceeding in which a criminal defendant is brought to court, told of the charges, and asked to plead guilty or not guilty.

BAIL: The temporary release of a person from jail when awaiting trial, on condition that a sum of money be lodged or deposited to guarantee an appearance in court.

BARRISTER: A lawyer admitted to plead at the Bar and who may try cases in superior court.

BURDEN OF PROOF: The duty to prove disputed facts.

CAUSE OF ACTION: A legal claim in a civil action.

COMPLAINT: A written statement that begins a civil lawsuit in which the plaintiff details the claims.

CONTRACT: An agreement between two or more persons to do something or to not do something.

CONVICTION: A judgment of guilt against a person charged with a crime.

CUSTOMS DUTY: A tariff or tax imposed on goods when transported across international borders.

COURT LIAISON: A person that coordinates with attorneys to perform administrative duties, such as scheduling witnesses, sharing information with law enforcement, and overseeing the reporting of cases to foreign embassies when applicable.

DAMAGES: Money that a defendant pays to a plaintiff in a civil case if the plaintiff wins.

DEFENDANT: 1) The individual against whom a civil claim is filed; 2) The individual against whom a criminal claim is filed.

FELONY: A serious crime, punishable by more than one year in prison.

MAGISTRATE: A judicial officer of a district court, who conducts initial proceedings in criminal cases, decides criminal misdemeanor cases, conducts many pretrial civil and criminal matters on behalf of district judges, and decides civil cases with the consent of the parties.

MISDEMEANOR: An offense punishable by one year or less in jail.

PLAINTIFF: A person or business that files a formal complaint with the court.

PLEA: In a criminal case, the answer of "guilty," "not guilty," or "no contest" in response to a criminal charge.

SOLICITOR: A lawyer who advises clients, represents them in lower court, and prepares cases for barristers to try in higher courts.

SOVEREIGN IMMUNITY: A legal doctrine by which the sovereign or the state (i.e. government) cannot commit a legal wrong and thus, it is immune from criminal and civil liability and cannot be sued.

STATUTE: A written law passed by a legislative body.

STATUTE OF LIMITATIONS: A statute prescribing a period of limitation to bring certain types of legal actions. If the action is not brought within that time, the person or entity (in a criminal context) is permanently barred from suing in court.

SUBPOENA: A command, issued under court authority, for a witness to appear and to give testimony.

TESTIMONY: Evidence presented orally by witnesses.

VERDICT: The decision of a judge or jury in a case.

WARRANT: Court authorization to conduct a search or to make an arrest.

ACKNOWLEDGMENTS

This book series would never have seen the light of day without the able assistance of the following people:

Kathy Adams, my paralegal for over 22 years, who is the "Best" I've ever worked with during my entire legal career because of her amazing work ethic, organizational skills, and her ability to think outside of the box in unique and creative ways;

Ally Knez-Siddique, a professional writer, and one of my paralegals, whose eye for detail, according to her, is both a blessing and a curse;

Gino Ibanez, my former law clerk, whose exceptional research skills helped move this book series along in its early stages;

Rosa Diaz Graham, my legal assistant who helped with research and word processing at the very beginning of this project;

Shelia Martin, one of my former paralegals, worked diligently on this series of books, even after taking on another job. Her organizational skills are reflected throughout;

Mindy Scarlett, my marketing and publishing "Guru"! Her creativity and vision have no boundaries!

ABOUT THE AUTHOR

Michael L. Moore practices in Orlando, Florida, the city where he spent his formative years. He credits the trauma of having his brother murdered when he was only 10 years old, as the catalyst that drew him into the practice of law.

Moore attended Florida State University, where he was a member of the FSU debate team. Upon graduating, he was awarded a full scholarship to attend the University of Tennessee College of Law, where he was elected President of the Student Bar Association. He further honed his advocacy and public speaking skills by participating in 'moot court' competitions.

After clerking at the Tennessee Attorney General's office while in law school, Moore moved back to Orlando, Florida, to work at the State Attorney's Office as a prosecutor, and where he was fortunate enough to meet the young lady that would eventually become his wife. Moore moved on to working for private law firms, both local and national, and eventually established his own law firm in 1999. He continues to make Orlando his home base.

It was the murder of a close friend and client in Jamaica that caused Moore to realize that books on laws in other countries were few and far between, and he was inspired to create Law of the Land Publishing. Moore launched Law of the Land Publishing to provide a series of guidebooks and a membership site for tourists and business travelers to stay up to date on the laws in each country they travel to, as well as having access to assistance if they run into legal issues.

"My vision is to educate people on what their legal rights are, and how they can access legal assistance, no matter where they have to travel to in the world," said Moore. "As Americans, we have a right to due process, but in some countries, you don't even have the right to access a square meal when incarcerated. My goal is to provide the information needed to stay out of trouble, as well as having access to assistance if trouble finds you."

www.ingramcontent.com/pod-product-compliance
Lightning Source LLC
Chambersburg PA
CBHW071719120626
46550CB00001B/304